Advance Praise for *Flying Off Everest*

"As Babu, Lakpa, and Costello so eloquently illustrate, you don't need oodles of sponsors, money, or gear to pull off your wildest dreams, no matter how zany. All you need is the uncompromising desire to see them through."

—EUGENE BUCHANAN,
AUTHOR OF *BROTHERS ON THE BASHKAUS*
AND FORMER EDITOR IN CHIEF OF *PADDLER* MAGAZINE

"Flying Off Everest features two dirt-poor Nepalese lads who are impossible not to root for as they attempt a ridiculously bold and unrealistic adventure. Along the way we learn lots about Nepal, Everest, Sherpas, and more. Costello, a serious outdoorsman and a skilled journalist, tells us how they reached the highest point on earth and why they were so determined to fly and paddle to a destination beyond the wildest dreams of most of us. An inspiring tale that happens to be a great read."

—JOE GLICKMAN, AUTHOR OF *FEARLESS*

"A book worthy of inclusion in the travel-writing pantheon."
—JEFF JACKSON, EDITOR OF *ROCK & ICE* MAGAZINE

FLYING OFF EVEREST

A Journey from the Summit to the Sea

DAVE COSTELLO

LYONS PRESS
Guilford, Connecticut
An imprint of Globe Pequot Press

To buy books in quantity for corporate use
or incentives, call **(800) 962-0973**
or e-mail **premiums@GlobePequot.com.**

Lyons Press is an imprint of Globe Pequot Press.

Map by Melissa Baker © Morris Book Publishing, LLC
Editor: Katie Benoit
Project editor: Meredith Dias
Layout: Melissa Evarts

Library-of-Congress Cataloging-in-Publication Data is available on file.

ISBN 978-0-7627-8966-5

Printed in the United States of America

10 9 8 7 6 5 4 3 2 1

Author's Note

The people and events portrayed in this book are real. All descriptions are based on photographs and/or video, site visits, and interviews with the individuals who were actually present during the events described. Interviews were conducted with witnesses separately and, when possible, together. When multiple versions of a story existed, I chose the interpretations that best fit the verifiable facts. I have tried to be clear, within the text itself, what is speculation and what supports that speculation. All direct quotes and dialogue came from either recorded interviews or film footage from the actual expedition. No one included in this book was asked for exclusivity to his or her story.

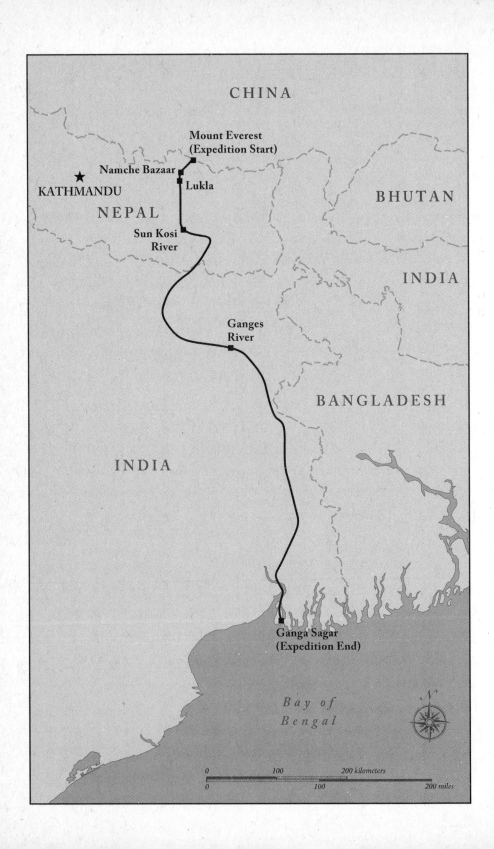

CHINA

Mount Everest
(Expedition Start)

Namche Bazaar

Lukla

KATHMANDU

NEPAL

BHUTAN

Sun Kosi
River

INDIA

Ganges
River

BANGLADESH

INDIA

Ganga Sagar
(Expedition End)

Bay of
Bengal

N

| 0 | 100 | 200 kilometers |
| 0 | 100 | 200 miles |

Contents

Dramatis Personae

Listed alphabetically by first name

Alex Treadway—Freelance photographer/videographer for *National Geographic Adventure.*

Balkrishna Basel (Baloo)—Babu's friend; trekked paraglider to Everest Base Camp.

Charley Gaillard—Owner of the Ganesh Kayak Shop, expedition sponsor.

David Arrufat—Swiss paragliding pilot, owner of Blue Sky Paragliding, cofounder of the Association of Paragliding Pilots and Instructors (APPI), expedition sponsor.

Hamilton Pevec—American filmmaker, editor/director of *Hanuman Airlines.*

Kelly Magar—Co-owner of Paddle Nepal, Nim Magar's wife, expedition sponsor.

Kili Sherpa—Owner of High Altitude Dreams, Lakpa Tsheri Sherpa's cousin.

Kimberly Phinney (Ruppy)—American fashion designer, expedition sponsor.

Krishna Sunuwar—Babu's younger brother, expedition safety kayaker on the Sun Kosi and Ganges.

Lakpa Tsheri Sherpa—Babu's expedition partner, mountain guide, sherpa.

Madhukar Pahari—Expedition support raft oarsman on the Sun Kosi, Paddle Nepal employee.

Nim Magar—Co-owner of Paddle Nepal, expedition sponsor.

Nima Wang Chu—Expedition sherpa, trekking guide.

Pete Astles—British professional kayaker, expedition sponsor; shipped paddling gear from the United Kingdom for use on the expedition.

Phu Dorji Sherpa (Ang Bhai)—Expedition sherpa, trekking guide.

Resham Bahadur Thapa—Expedition safety kayaker on the Sun Kosi.

Ryan Waters—American climber/mountain guide, owner of Mountain Professionals; shared Base Camp with Babu and Lakpa's team.

Sano Babu Sunuwar (Babu)—Lakpa Tsheri Sherpa's expedition partner, paragliding pilot, kayaker.

Shri Hari Shresthra—Expedition cameraman.

Susmita Rai—Babu's wife.

Tsering Nima—Owner of Himalayan Trailblazer, expedition sponsor.

Wildes Antonioli (Mukti)—David Arrufat's girlfriend.

Yanjee Sherpa—Lakpa's wife.

From where the water begins, at the supreme source, to where it divides into egos and has separate names; to where the water unites with all rivers to become one with the ocean.

—SANO BABU SUNUWAR

And this I believe: that the free, exploring mind of the individual human is the most valuable thing in the world.

—JOHN STEINBECK, *EAST OF EDEN*

PROLOGUE

The Northeast Summit Ridge of Mount Everest, May 21, 2011—28,896 feet

A step forward there is a 10,000-foot drop into Tibet. Two men stand on a small patch of snow, looking down the North Face of Mount Everest. Waiting. Heel to toe. Connected at the waist by a pair of carabiners. They say nothing, listening to the wind whistling in their ears. Behind them lies a fluttering red and white nylon tandem paragliding wing, and another cliff. The 11,000-foot Kangshung Face. They know that jumping off the top of the world will mark only the beginning of the much longer, more audacious journey that they have planned all the way to the sea. And that flying off Everest in what is essentially a large kite should actually be the easiest part.

Lakpa, who is standing in front, nearest to the edge, looks at his watch. It reads 9:40 a.m. He and his climbing partner, Babu, a professional paragliding pilot and kayaker who has climbed only once before now, have been on top of the world for over an hour. They have not slept in two days. Standing at the edge of the troposphere, their oxygen-deprived brains are struggling to stay conscious—let alone think clearly about launching a paraglider at roughly the cruising altitude of a jetliner. Wearing crampons. The few, strained mouthfuls of warm noodles they forced themselves to eat the night before at Camp IV on the Southeast Ridge have long since vanished. However, they are not hungry. Above 26,000 feet, in the "Death Zone," where life cannot sustain itself for more than a few days, at most, their bodies prefer to eat themselves.

Babu, a head shorter than Lakpa and standing directly behind him, is praying, dressed in a red and blue full-body down suit, an old, orange, sticker-encrusted helmet on his head. They need the wind, which is gusting up to 30 miles per hour, to stop. *For just twenty minutes,* Babu suggests quietly to the heavens. It's how long he estimates they will need to fly off the mountain, down to the airstrip at Namche Bazaar, 18 miles and 17,743 vertical feet away.

Lakpa, wearing a yellow-orange and black one-piece down suit and an old blue skateboarding helmet decorated with a sticker of the Nepali flag, is having difficulties breathing. His head is reeling. His vision is dimming. Later, he will describe this moment as "critical." For now, though, he tries not to fall over. They are down to one bottle of oxygen, which Babu is inhaling at a rapid rate. Lakpa, who has summited Everest three times before now, has turned Babu's regulator on full flow. He figures it will be best for both of them if his friend stays as conscious as possible during the flight. Babu is the pilot, after all. And Lakpa can hardly fly a paraglider, even at low altitude. He just started learning to fly.

Allowing his gaze to drift over the horizon as he prays, Babu can feel the hard granules of icy snow blowing in the wind, hitting his face. Clouds roll slowly through the lesser mountains to the north. The air above is flawless cobalt.

A white ocean under blue sky.

Nima Wang Chu, one of only two young, high-altitude sherpas hired to help carry loads for the small, four-man, all-Nepali climbing team, sits unroped close to the other side of the narrow, gently sloping Northeast Summit Ridge. A few feet of overhanging corniced snow separates him from an abrupt descent down the Kangshung Face. He is clutching the nylon wing attached to Lakpa and Babu to the ground, trying his best to keep the 51-foot sail from catching in the wind. A low-altitude trekking guide back home in the Khumbu Valley, he also has been climbing only once before now. Phu Dorji (called "Ang Bhai"), the other young climbing sherpa in the group, is just a few yards farther down the ridge, crouching behind a boulder and holding a small video camera. He's the only one in the group attached to a rope—and likewise has no technical climbing experience.

The team only has enough food and oxygen left for two of them to make the two-day return journey to Base Camp. Unless the wind stops, Babu and Lakpa will have to descend without the aid of supplemental oxygen and face the inevitable bottleneck of climbers, guides, and sherpas climbing and descending on a "nice day" above Camp IV on Mount Everest.

They also think they will lose their chance to become the first people to paraglide off the summit of Mount Everest, the goal that had prompted them to plan their expedition in less than six months in the first place.

What Babu and Lakpa don't know is that the feat that they think they're about to attempt, and claim for Nepal, has already been done. Twice. A simple online search using the keywords "paragliding off Everest" would have told them about French paragliding pilot Jean-Marc Boivin's initial record-setting solo flight from the summit in 1988, as well as the French couple Zebulon and Claire Bernier Roche's successful tandem flight from the top of Everest in 2001. However, Babu and Lakpa didn't do an Internet search before climbing the world's tallest mountain and paragliding off of it. They've never heard of Boivin or the Roches.

Back on the summit, forty-two-year-old Benegas Brothers expedition leader Damian Benegas watches the unlikely Nepali crew prepare for their flight, along with his two clients: ESPN Latin Ad Sales executive Leonardo McLean and Argentinian climber Matias Erroz. Each of them has extensive high-altitude mountaineering experience on nearly every continent. And each has paid approximately $65,000 to be a part of the first all-Argentinian climbing team to reach the top of Everest, which they accomplished that morning—with the help of hired sherpas.

None of the climbers on top of Everest that day have any idea that, after flying off of the summit, the two Nepali men standing on the ridge in front of them are going to continue on to fly south across the Himalaya and kayak nearly 400 miles on the Sun Kosi and Ganges Rivers out to the Bay of Bengal. That it will take them over a month. That they will be arrested, robbed, and nearly drowned. Repeatedly.

Then, as if on cue, the wind stops.

It's the tremendously unlikely, and likely brief, break in the weather that they've been waiting for—and desperately counting on—for over an hour. Babu barely has enough oxygen left to last the flight. "No problem," he says to Lakpa, smiling. He imagines himself somewhere else—a green, grassy foothill near his home in central Nepal, with a warm, gentle breeze—and signals for Nima Wang Chu to lift the wing.

"Run," he tells Lakpa. Firmly. Without yelling.

They both know they are either going to fly off the mountain or die.

Part I

The Ascent

I

Small Child

It appeared suddenly, like an animal moving toward him along the road. Fast. A long, lingering trail of dust rose from its tracks. Enormous, unlike anything the boy had ever seen. A loud, constant rumble echoed through the mountains. *Like rocks falling, which never stop*, he thought. Then he saw the people inside.

"Oh, shit," Babu said.

Fifteen-year-old Sano Babu Sunuwar didn't realize it was the bus that would take him to Kathmandu. He had never seen a bus before. He had never seen anything with wheels. Not even a bicycle. It was the first time he had stood on the side of a road. Anywhere. He was barefoot and carried no bag. Everything he owned was in his pocket: 500 rupees—about $5—given to him by his father a few days before, after Babu graduated from tenth grade, the highest level of school offered anywhere near his family's village. It was a three-day walk along the river back to his home, which he had never left before, until then. This was also the first time he had had money. Ever. His friend, standing next to him, who had been to the capital city once before and had promised to help find him a job there, prompted him to get on the bus and hand over his newfound wealth to the man collecting fares. The fare collector gave him the equivalent of $2 back. It was a four-hour ride through the mountains to Kathmandu on a single-lane dirt road.

Babu was running away. To what, he wasn't sure.

He was born the eldest of two sons on May 30, 1983, just south of Everest and the Solu-Khumbu region in the remote eastern Nepali hill village of Rampur-6.* Babu's first name, Sano, means "small" in English. No one calls him this, though he has always been small, even at birth. Because of his bright, happy brown eyes and contagious toothy grin, his friends and family quickly took to calling him by his middle name, Babu, which in Nepali is a term of endearment for a young boy or "child"—even once he was no longer a child. His surname, Sunuwar, denotes his family's ethnicity. Completely separate, but vaguely similar to the nearby Sherpa clans to the north, the Sunuwar are part of a larger ethnic group known as the Rais, whose origins lie in Mongolia but who have their own unique language and religion, predating both Buddhism and Hinduism. Farmers and fishermen, they have carved a life for themselves out of the forested foothills beneath the mountains for thousands of years, hand-digging row upon row of narrow terraces to grow rice, millet, and barley, casting their hand-stitched nets into the white rivers that flow and rage beneath the world's tallest mountains.

The village of Rampur-6 sits along the banks of the Sun Kosi River, high on a ridge. The river below is deep and wide, and blue green, except during the monsoon, when it swells over its banks, churning dark orange-brown, thick with alluvial silt. The hillsides, rising steeply from either side, are covered in a dense green forest. Blue pine, juniper, fir, birch, rhododendron, bamboo, barberry. The jungle teems with thars, spotted deer, langur, monkeys, mountain foxes, and martins. Blood pheasant, red-billed and alpine chough, and Himalayan monal.

---

* Under the current Nepali system of government, individual villages are known as "wards." They typically are numbered one through nine and grouped together with other nearby communities into slightly larger Village Development Committees (VDCs). So Babu's family lives in Ward 6 of the Rampur VDC.

Snow leopards prowl higher in the mountains to the north, above the snow line, hunting blue sheep.

Six miles to the west, the Tamba Kosi finds its end after tumbling out of the high Himalaya at the mouth of a deep canyon. To the east lie the confluences of the Likhu Khola, the Majhigau Khola, and the infamous Dudh Kosi, the highest-elevation river in the world, which crashes through the mountains from the base of Mount Everest at a rate of roughly 600 feet per mile.

A narrow dirt path winds down around the ridge to the bottom of the pine forest, where a small creek flows into the broad, swiftly moving river. The path picks up again on the other side of the current, zigzagging its way up and over the adjacent hills into the next valley. During Babu's childhood there were no bridges, no roads.*

The home he ran away from was, essentially, the same as all of the others in Rampur-6. A thatch roof covered a narrow, two-story structure held together with logs, rope, and dried mud. Half was built with uneven stones collected from the terraced hillsides below. The other half was open to the air, a simple covered wooden platform that served as a sort of deck and an extension of the house, which, in effect, nearly doubled its size. The first level had three walls and a dirt floor and acted as the family's barn. Cows and goats ruminated in the shade on grass grown on the steep hillside below, brought up the ridge for them by foot, usually by Babu. Up a short ladder was a small, windowless room—the family's main living area. There was a shallow recess in the floor for cooking fires, but no chimney. The smoke collected thickly on the ceiling. A doorless doorway led out to the second-story platform, which was covered by the thatch roof and open on three sides. Hay dried slowly on a head-high wooden rack. There were no chairs, no furniture. Listless bent dogs and thin chickens wandered aimlessly outside.

Babu's father was a fisherman. Early each morning he would walk forty-five minutes down the ridgeline to the river, where he would fish,

---

* There is now a single-lane dirt road running along the length of most of the Sun Kosi, as well as a small suspension footbridge connecting the trail to Rampur-6 to the new road.

often until dark. He taught his son how to swim in the cold waters of the Sun Kosi, how to move with the swirling currents and survive in a whitewater rapid, should the boy ever find himself unfortunate enough to fall into any of the surrounding rivers. Young Babu loved it, however, and soon began swimming the nearby Class IV* rapid with his friends, but without a personal flotation device (PFD)—on purpose. It was one of the few things he and the other boys his age did for fun. "Everything else was for survival," Babu says. "Not fun." At the age of twelve, he watched one of his friends drown while swimming in the rapids. Babu continued swimming.

As a child Babu was kept busy carrying hay for the cows and goats up the steep ridge from the terraced fields that his mother and he tended while his father fished. He watched after the animals as they grazed in the forest, and he completed a long list of other daily tasks that go along with subsistence living in the mountains in Nepal. If he didn't do his chores, his mother didn't feed him, he says. Two meals a day of either fire-roasted fish or *dal bhat*, a spicy rice and lentil dish with roasted potatoes, and sometimes yak meat or beef—usually not.

After completing his morning chores, collecting milk and carrying hay, Babu would walk to school. It took him twenty-five minutes to get to the small, government-funded Level 1 school in his village. It offered classes up to Grade 3. He attended whenever he could, when his parents didn't need his help at home, which was rare. After completing third grade, young Babu started making the forty-five-minute trek to the nearest Level 2 school. His main goal was to learn how to

---

* In kayaking or rafting, whitewater rapids are typically divided into six classes, each denoted with a Roman numeral. Class I is moving flat water with a few small waves; it is straightforward to navigate in a boat. Class II is relatively small rapids; waves up to three feet; and wide, clear channels that are still somewhat easy to navigate. Class III is rapids with high, irregular waves and narrow routes through hazards. It often requires complex maneuvering to navigate in a boat. Class IV is difficult rapids with restricted passages, requiring precise maneuvering in turbulent water. Conditions often make rescue difficult. Class V is extremely difficult, long, and violent rapids. Rescue conditions are exceedingly difficult, and there is a significant hazard to life in the event of a mishap. Class VI is typically considered unrunnable.

read and write, which proved difficult in a school with no books. After completing sixth grade, it was an hour walk each way to his Level 3 school, which went to eighth grade. No lunch was offered during the day. He ate in the morning and at night, if he finished his chores. And that was becoming increasingly difficult with his now two-hour walking commute to school. The nearest Level 4 school, the highest offered, was in a neighboring village called Dudbhanjyang, across the river and over a small mountain.

Babu crossed the Sun Kosi Monday through Friday just after dawn on an old, inflated tractor tire inner tube that had been carried in from the nearest road, a three-day walk away. He didn't even know what a tractor looked like. It took three hours, one way, gaining and losing 1,000 feet of elevation in each direction. He carried a notebook and a pencil, supplied to him by the school. The high school itself, which sat on top of a similarly narrow and inconveniently accessible ridge in the next valley, consisted of two long stone buildings covered in cracking white plaster, with red wooden roofs and cold, bare concrete floors. The windows held no glass. The teacher would have to close the red wooden shutters to keep out the wind and rain, making the classroom, lacking electricity, eerily dark. Unlike most of his classmates, whose parents often kept them at home to help with farming and chores, Babu managed to complete tenth grade, the final year offered, at the age of fifteen. He knew how to read and write in Nepali, making him one of the 54.1 percent of Nepalese who could at the time.[*] And yet he had nothing to read.

The idea to leave the village came from the river. Standing on the riverbank or high on a ridge, doing his chores or walking to and from school, Babu often saw strange things float past, bobbing in the waves. They would always be brightly colored. Blue. Red. Yellow. Green. The floating things were odd, he thought, but it was the people on top, or sitting inside of them, that captivated Babu's imagination the most.

---

[*] According to Nepal's 2001 National Census. That number has since jumped to 65.9 percent, according to the 2011 National Census.

They were kayakers. Whitewater rafters. Foreigners with light-colored skin who spoke strange languages. English. Chinese. French. He didn't know anything about them, other than that they came from upriver somewhere and went downriver to . . . well, somewhere else—someplace far from where he was. "That's all I knew," he says. He would watch them from his family's house, as they rested on the riverbank below, drying wetsuits, napping, playing games in the sand. He imagined what it would be like to be one of them. Not having to milk cows and goats each morning. Not having to carry hay or walk three hours to school each way. To just step into the river each day with a small, happy-colored boat with a big stick, and float downstream to something new. Playing in the water. Following the river. *That must be a good life,* he thought. *Maybe the best life.* Certainly better than the one he was living at the moment, he thought. So Babu began to dream of kayaking and a new life of adventure.

When Babu graduated from school, his father gave him some money to attend the graduation feast put on each year by the high school in Dudbhanjyang: 500 rupees. It was the first time Babu had ever had money in his possession. He knew the small wad of papers that his father pressed into his hands was an opportunity, though. And not just an opportunity to eat well and get drunk, which was the intended purpose. It was his ticket out of the hills, a chance at a new beginning, one without goats or cows or the job of carrying hay. *Perhaps even a chance to go kayaking,* he thought.

Babu consulted an older friend who had made the trip out of the hills once before and had returned after working for some years in Kathmandu, the country's capital. They made a plan, which started simply enough with walking into the hills and out of the village, without telling their parents. Away from everything Babu had ever known. Then, they would catch this thing called a "bus," his friend told him, that would take them to the city. Babu would learn how to kayak—somewhere, somehow—and convince somebody to pay him for it. A few days later, when it was finally time for the graduation feast, they said good-bye to their families, without telling them of their plan; crossed the wide blue-green river using the old inner tubes left on the bank for the purpose, past the dirt trail that led up the opposing hill-side to Dudbhanjyang and their graduation party; and kept walking westward over white stones. Three days through the forest, along the river to the road.

Babu knew it was not a safe time to be traveling. Nepal was three years into a civil war. People left their villages only if they had to, because when they did, they tended to disappear.

On February 13, 1996, when Babu was just twelve years old, members of the Communist Party of Nepal attacked police posts all over the country. The guerillas, led by a man named Pushpa Kamal Dahal, who called himself Prachanda, killed the officers and took their weapons, hoarding them for future attacks in what he accurately anticipated was going to be a long, bloody struggle for control of Nepal. It was the beginning of what would turn into a horrific ten-year civil war—"the People's War," Prachanda called it. The conflict would eventually cost more than 12,800 lives and displace over 150,000 Nepalese from their homes. The economy crashed. Unemployment reached nearly 50 percent, the country left, for all practical purposes, in ruin.

For hundreds of years, ten generations of the Shah dynasty had ruled Nepal, as either an absolute monarchy or a constitutional monarchy, constitutionally immune to prosecution. The Maoists, Nepalis loyal to the now infamous Communist Chinese revolutionary/tyrant Mao Zedong, claimed that Nepal's rulers had failed to bring genuine democracy and development to the people of Nepal, which was true. In the eighteenth century, members of the Shah family had cut off the lips of their challengers. A hundred years later, they were dropping uncooperative subjects down wells. More recently, a member of the royal family had allegedly run over a musician on the street with his Mitsubishi Pajero. The man hadn't played his request.

The day-to-day economics and development of Nepal also hadn't gone so well for the Shahs. By 1996, 71 percent of Nepal's population was living on less than $1 a day—absolute poverty. More than half of the people in Nepal were illiterate. And foreign debt accounted for at least 60 percent of the country's gross domestic product. Even today, Nepal is still listed as one of the twenty poorest countries in the world by the United Nations, just ahead of Uganda and Haiti.

The communists promised to empower the people, redistribute the country's wealth, grant women equal rights, and eliminate the Hindu caste system, which had been "officially" adopted by Nepal during a period of absolute monarchy between 1960 and 1990. The Maoists looted police stations for weapons and made homemade explosives, preparing for the long guerilla siege to come. As the conflict escalated they began invading remote villages like Babu's, which were unprotected by the royal army, barging into classrooms, shooting teachers and abducting the pupils, forcing them to fight as child soldiers. They tortured their opponents and exhibited their mutilated bodies in the streets. They had lost their cause, but continued fighting.

In 2001 the Nepali Parliament passed the Terrorist and Destructive Activities Act, allowing ninety-day detentions and the unapologetically forceful interrogation of known Maoists. King Gyanendra suspended the elected government and instituted martial law, effectively controlling the military and the press.

Babu, like most people in the country who scratched a subsistence living off the land, was rightly afraid of both the government and the insurgents. He didn't know whom to trust, if he must, and that the answer was probably neither the Maoists nor the government. He was on his own, and he knew it.

Once in Kathmandu, Babu's friend immediately got him a job working in a carpet factory. He spent anywhere from twelve to twenty hours a day, seven days a week, working along with dozens of other teenage boys and girls, sitting in a small, crowded room. According to Babu, his payment was 200 rupees per month ($2), two meals of dal bhat a day, and a space on the floor inside the factory on which to sleep. His friend had gone and had not returned. Babu was alone.

This, of course, was not what he had been hoping for when he had left home. He was accomplishing nothing, he thought. He was frustrated. So after two months of mind-numbing, tedious labor, Babu quit, with almost no money and no place to stay.

Babu slept on the streets in cold, dark corners until he found his next job, working as a bus assistant. This new position required him to stand in the aisle of the bus and collect fares all day, and to clean it each night—sweeping, picking up trash, dealing with belligerent passengers who were unwilling or unable to pay. It was the easiest thing young Babu had ever done in his life, and it paid, respectively, in spades: 500 rupees a month, and 100 rupees per day for food. He ate well: two meals of dal bhat each day, every day. It also afforded him the opportunity to sleep on the bus. After twenty-six days Babu had managed to save over 1,000 rupees ($10), all the money he had earned that he hadn't spent on food.

He bought a bus ticket back to the nearest road to his village and walked three days along the river home, proud to have doubled the money his father had originally given him for his graduation present. His parents, although glad to see him and more than happy to have the unexpected extra income he gave them, didn't want him to go back to the city. They asked Babu to remain in the village. Yet, just a few months later, in January 2000, Babu returned to Kathmandu again, this time with no money. His grandfather had needed help herding cows to a neighboring village, and after helping him move the cattle, Babu simply kept walking to the road and caught another bus back to the city. This time he was looking for a job in the tourism industry, which he had learned, during his time working on the bus, was the real moneymaking business to be in. Besides, he still wanted to learn how to kayak. So he went where the tourists go: Thamel.

Located on the north side of Kathmandu, Thamel occupies less than 1 square mile of the city. Yet it is the sightseeing hub of Nepal, housing nearly all of the country's adventure tourism companies, upscale hotels, and restaurants that serve everything from pizza to steak and apple pie. The streets are narrow, winding, and categorically confusing, built in a time before cars and, evidently, reason. There are no sidewalks. Tucked between old, close-fitting buildings that tower up to seven stories overhead, it's like walking through a small, urban canyon: more often in shadow than not, even on a sunny day. Crowds of people, scooters, motorcycles, and cars all navigate the tiny alleys, darting beneath innumerable signs covering the walls, directing people to businesses that oftentimes no longer exist. Or perhaps have just moved locations, without bothering to remove the sign from their old whereabouts. Standing in front of their shops, vendors call out to passersby, hoping to lure them into a sale by yelling louder than anyone else. A collective cacophony, advertising everything from a simple loaf of bread to a multiday rafting trip down the Karnali, rises up from the smog. The sound of motorcycle and scooter horns regularly punctuates the dissonance. Small children in tattered clothes and lepers crawling on the ground ask for change, speaking English.

Upon arriving in Thamel, Babu saw some men loading equipment into a line of trucks: backpacks, portable stoves, tents, food. He approached them and politely asked, "Where is this trekking equipment going?"

"Pokhara," one of the men told him.

Babu had heard of Pokhara before, during his last visit to Kathmandu. He knew that, like Thamel, it was a place tourists often went. And that it was a popular place for whitewater kayaking and rafting in Nepal. At least, that's what he had heard. He had never been there, and he didn't know anyone who had been there either.

"Do you need a porter?" Babu asked.

"Have you done trekking before?" one of the men loading the truck probed.

"Yes," Babu said without hesitating. He knew if he told the truth— that he had never worked as a porter before in his life—they would never take him. He spent the day helping the men load their trucks for the expedition. They gave him no food or water. As the afternoon wore on, Babu began to wonder where he would sleep that night if they didn't take him along. They hadn't told him yes, but they hadn't told him no. He was hungry and thirsty. At the end of the day, when the trucks were finally full and as the sun was setting, one of the men put 20 rupees in his hand. "Thank you for helping," he said. "But we cannot take you with us. You are too small." With that, the men got into the trucks and left.

Babu walked to the bus station. He asked the man working at the counter how much a ticket to Pokhara cost. The man told him it was 150 rupees. The last bus scheduled to leave Kathmandu that night departed at 9:00 p.m. and was expected to arrive in Pokhara at around 4:00 a.m. the next day. Unable to afford the fare, Babu waited, watching the people loading and unloading as it grew dark. He watched quietly as the last bus turned on its engine and slowly began to roll away. He looked around. Then, when he saw that no one was looking, he ran and jumped through the door, onto the bus.

Babu found himself seated next to an old man holding crutches. Babu could see that the man had only one leg. He looked ragged and disheveled. Destitute, just like him. The old man, having watched Babu's desperate leap onto the bus, asked him how much money he had.

"Twenty rupees," Babu told him truthfully.

"Do you know how much a ticket costs to Pokhara?" the old man asked.

"The counter price is 150 rupees," Babu admitted sheepishly.

"Yes, yes," the old man said. "Now here's an idea: They can see that I have only one leg and will feel sorry for me. But you, you have everything they can see. So if I tell them you cannot speak, you must not speak. When people come to collect money, I will tell them that I have no leg and that you cannot speak." Babu, having no better alternative, agreed to follow the plan. The bus bumped and swayed on the broken road. Outlines of dimly lit buildings passed slowly through dark, dusty windows.

Babu could see the bus assistant looking at him and the old man, obviously concerned, as he collected fares from the other passengers. Babu had done the man's job himself, and he knew what was coming.

"Hey, you two," the young man finally said as he reached their seats. "Where are you going?"

Babu, not actually knowing sign language, raised his hands and wiggled his fingers with imagined meaning. The old man waited a moment for the uncomfortable display to finish, then spoke.

"We are going Pokhara because we have trouble," he said. "This boy is my friend. He cannot speak. We don't have money." The statement hung in the air, shuddering along with the bus as it jostled itself noisily over the cracks in the road. Babu put his hands down.

"You don't have money?" the assistant asked, alarmed. "Why did you come to Kathmandu then? Why didn't you just stay in Pokhara?"

"We wanted to come to see our relatives," the old man said simply. "But we cannot find them. So we have to go back." The bus assistant thought about this for a moment, considering the difficulties involved with stopping the bus and throwing an old man with one leg and a mute boy out onto the street at night. The other passengers would not be pleased, he knew. He then turned and continued to walk down the aisle, collecting fares, leaving Babu and the old man to sit together in silence.

Through the windows, Babu watched the silhouettes of Kathmandu's tall brick buildings slowly turn to vague outlines of dark roadside shacks. Sheet metal roofs held down by old discarded tires, rocks, and bricks. The mountains in the distance became distinguishable from the starry sky only by their darker blackness—a series of jagged holes in the horizon. The bus, rattling, climbed steeply out of the valley to the west and then crested over a narrow pass, dropping suddenly, clinging to the sides of the shadowed mountains, turning sharply, back and forth. Switching back on itself as it descended rapidly down to the Trisuli River and into the even deeper night of the valley below.

Hours later, the bus rolled to a stop in the small roadside town of Mugling, the halfway point between Kathmandu and Pokhara. Babu rose stiffly from his seat, exiting the bus for a scheduled thirty-minute bathroom and dal bhat break. The town was dark and still, save the lone roadside vendor who had stayed open to serve the passengers on the last bus to Pokhara that night. The old man with one leg immediately began to beg for food, asking the other passengers to buy him and his young friend a meal. Babu hadn't eaten in almost two days and so didn't find it prudent to discourage him.

"Can your friend work?" someone asked, pointing to Babu.

"Yes! Yes! Yes!" the old man replied, ready to volunteer him for any sort of labor that might get them both some food. Babu knew he was too weak and malnourished to work, so he began to wave his hands wildly, making recognizably desperate gestures in the half-light of the bus stop. He placed his left palm up in front of him, like a plate, and mimed the motion of eating dal bhat, pinching the imaginary soggy lentils and rice between his fingers and shoveling them greedily into his open mouth. It was pathetic, he knew, but the display had the desired effect. Babu and the old man ate their free meals quickly and got back on the bus, completely silent.

At 4:00 a.m. Babu stepped down onto the gravel parking lot of the Pokhara bus station for the first time. The city was quiet, the morning air still cool and dark, waiting for the sun to rise and glare off the whiteness of the mountains in the distance. In his pocket he still had the 20 rupees (about 20 cents) he earned helping load trucks back in Kathmandu. Looking around the vacant lot and the surrounding darkness, he realized, suddenly, that he had absolutely no idea where he was, where he was going, or what he was going to do next.

He asked someone walking by, "Do you know where I can find the tourists?"

II

The Flying Sherpa

Sarangkot, Nepal,
November 2010—Approximately 2,925 Feet

"Run," Babu said, and watched as his new friend, Lakpa, sprinted toward the steep drop-off 20 feet in front of him. Below lay the terraced rice fields of Sarangkot, a small hillside village located 2.5 miles north of Pokhara that's not entirely unaccustomed to paragliders crashing into it. Pokhara is one of the best and most popular places in the world to go paragliding, and the crest of the hill above the small village of Sarangkot is the best and closest place to launch a paraglider from the city. On good days, when the sky is clear with a warm sun and no wind, the grassy hillside bustles with pilots and their tandem passengers and the sky above fills with a circling swarm of paragliders, rising up into the clouds and then sinking back down on the breeze. Beyond the fields to the south sits the growing expanse of the city and the dark blue of Lake Phewa.

Lakpa's paraglider wing caught the air and quickly began to rise. The large, 40-plus-foot sail pulled back at him. A few more hurried steps and suddenly the ground was out from under his feet. He was flying—*although not well*, Babu observed. Lakpa didn't actually know how to fly. Unlike the other pilots around him, who circled upward in the nearby thermal—a hot uprising of air beside the hill, like the swirling eddy that forms behind a rock in a river—Lakpa floated straight down toward the lake. He had flown only a handful of times before, first during a nine-day introduction course in Pokhara in 2009, and then again a few months later during a quick and mildly disastrous flight in the Khumbu, which resulted in him landing rather inelegantly in a tree. In Sarangkot he was the only pilot in the sky wearing a personal flotation device (PFD). Knowing he could land in the lake, Lakpa, who couldn't swim, borrowed the PFD just in case he overshot his landing site on the shore.

Babu considered this as he watched his new friend descend, and wondered why Lakpa, a well-paid Sherpa who made his living climbing mountains, would ever want to fly. *It is not normal*, he was certain. Babu waited to see how the landing went before making any decisions about sharing his plans for Everest with Lakpa. He didn't want a dead Sherpa on his conscience, certainly—but he also couldn't help but wonder if Lakpa might just be crazy enough to help him with his idea to fly off the top of the world. After all, Lakpa had already told him that he wanted to fly off all of the peaks he regularly guided on. And the man had already climbed Everest. Three times.

———

Pokhara, Nepal, November 2010—Approximately 2,625 Feet A few hours earlier . . .

The city of Pokhara is in central Nepal. The town sits on the eastern shore of Phewa Tal, a large lake in Pokhara Valley, which is a widening of the Seti Gandaki Valley just south of the 26,545-foot Annapurna Massif—a broad, gleaming white band of the Himalaya rising up from the forested foothills just outside of town. The Seti Gandaki River runs through Pokhara, its churning waters flowing through deep, cavernous gorges, often right beneath the city. A single two-lane mountain road called the Prithvi Highway follows the meandering banks of the nearby Trisuli River and its white, river-washed boulders out of town, connecting the city to the capital, Kathmandu, 126 miles to the east. By a rather remarkable orographical fluke—the combined interaction of the area's mountains, valleys, and the resulting paradise-like subtropical weather systems—it's also one of the best places in the world to go paragliding. Nearly every day of the year dozens, if not hundreds, of paragliders can be seen floating overhead—brightly colored, downward-curving crescents carving wide, deceptively lazy-looking circles in the sky.

In the daytime the narrow streets are filled with buses and trucks, cars and motorbikes—the squawk of their horns, the belch of exhaust—bicycles, pushcarts, horses and wheelbarrows, dogs, chickens, children, and trash, and tourists taking pictures of it all. In the morning, when the roads are quiet, before the sun is high and disperses the fog that settles in the valley each night and often lingers to midday, shopkeepers stoop in front of their open-air stores with short-handled brooms, sweeping the night's dust into the street. Some will later ask the foreign tourists who walk by on their way to Lakeside, on the north end of town, to "sponsor" them for a work visa out of the country, already knowing the answer (no), but still hoping, trying to escape the tourists' paradise.

Lakeside is a single street, a little over a mile long, that houses nearly all of the local adventure tourism companies, the most profitable businesses in town. They sell everything from guided trekking and rafting trips, to kayak and bike rentals, to tandem paragliding flights in which a trained vulture lands on a paying customer's outstretched arm in the sky. Most of the buildings have new-looking signs featuring large, color photographs of bright orange, red, and blue paragliding wings in flight, framed by the white teeth of the Annapurnas. Other displays feature smiling customers rafting, biking, hiking—sometimes even rappelling off waterfalls. In many places kayaks—old sun-bleached models, never new—line the sidewalks, blocking the footpath. Between the outfitters are restaurants with English-speaking waiters and signs that advertise American and Italian food (AMERICAN BREAKFAST! FIRE WOOD PIZZA!). The remaining structures are Westerner-friendly hotels that offer hot water, "expensive" $3.50 beers, and sit-down toilets. Foreign tourists call it the nice part of town.

At the end of Lakeside, on the left as one walked north toward the mountains, across the street from the Pokhara Pizza House, was the office of Blue Sky Paragliding, one of seventeen paragliding companies in the city. A large, hand-painted picture of Hanuman— a holy, flying monkey god and a popular member of the Hindu pantheon—adorned the sign hanging over the entrance. Propped up on an old tree stump out front stood a 6-foot-tall (fake) yeti, welcoming guests—mostly from Europe.* An old rooster crowed out back.

It was November—one of the two best months of the year (the other is December) for paragliding in Pokhara—and the Blue Sky Paragliding shop was busy. A man standing in line at the counter waited patiently to ask his question. It was the same question he had been asking all over Lakeside the past two months, at each of the paragliding shops, leaving repeated messages on their voice mails and sometimes even stopping strangers in the street to ask it.

He was tall for a Nepali: 5-foot-5. His boots were well worn beneath his faded black leather pants and brown leather motorcycle jacket. An army-green fighter pilot helmet, emblazoned with the red star of China, was tucked under his arm. He was not a communist; he simply liked the look of it. His eyes were dark brown and intelligent. On his chin sat a medium-length, well-kept goatee, and he had an impish grin.

---

* The offices of Blue Sky Paragliding moved in April 2013 to another location in the Lakeside area, farther south. The large picture of Hanuman is gone, but the yeti still stands watch near the entrance.

The young man working on the other side of the counter was clean-shaven and short, even for a Nepali. Strong, but boyish looking. "Hello," he said, his eyes also brown, but liquid and bright—gleaming like a child's. "My name is Babu."

The man in the motorcycle jacket quickly flashed a broad, white-toothed smile. "My name is Lakpa," he replied. "I'm looking for a secondhand wing."

Babu actually knew the stranger, and Lakpa knew Babu. They had, in fact, become friendly acquaintances on a rafting trip a year earlier. Babu, a lower-caste Sunuwar, was guiding the trip, and Lakpa, a relatively high-caste Sherpa, was on holiday, sent by his employer as a perk. They hadn't seen each other since.

Babu knew all too well how hard paragliding wings were to come by in Nepal—typically having to be bought from visiting foreigners to avoid the government's roughly 200 percent tax on all imported goods (hence all the old kayaks lining the streets of Pokhara). But what he heard next made him wonder if he should actually tell Lakpa he had an extra one, let alone sell it to him.

"I crashed mine into a tree, flying in the Solu-Khumbu," Lakpa said, still smiling. "I work as a climbing sherpa there, and I'm looking for a new one."

The Solu-Khumbu area, which lies just to the south of Everest in northeastern Nepal, is a dangerous place to fly, even for an experienced pilot. Babu knew this. It's filled with powerful updrafts and crosswinds, amidst some of the highest mountains in the world. Towering black cliffs line deep, narrow valleys covered in bristling conifers. There are plenty of hard, sharp places to crash into, which is the reason that people don't generally fly there and that the ones who do tend to get hurt. Babu had no idea whether Lakpa was an expert pilot or not. *He could just be an idiot*, he wondered.

"You didn't break anything?" Babu asked, a little surprised that Lakpa hadn't died. "Never do that again," he suggested warily, and then he recommended they take his old beginner wing out ground handling. That is to say, unfold it and see if Lakpa knew which end was up.

Neither of them knew the other was also thinking about flying off the top of the world's tallest mountain soon—or the other's remarkable backstory.

⌐ ⌐

Lakpa Tsheri Sherpa was born in Pokhara in 1976. His parents, Nima Nuru and Nima Phuti Sherpa,* who share a first name that means "Sunday" in English, named him Lhakpa,† or "Wednesday"——after the day on which he was born. Lovingly, they gave him the second name of "Long Life," or Tsheri.‡ A few years later, before Lakpa can even remember, they moved their family, including Lakpa's two older sisters, Nyima Yangji and Jangmu Lhamu, back to the family farm in Chaurikharka, south of Everest, where they soon had Lakpa's younger sister, Nyima Doma.

Chaurikharka is a small mountain village in northeastern Nepal, tucked into a green, forested hillside beneath the towering white peaks of the Solu-Khumbu region. Like all of the small villages in the remote 425-square-mile valley, it doesn't have an inch of paved road. There are no buses or cars. No bicycles. Everything from potatoes to the toilets that are brought in for the tourists that come to see and sometimes climb the surrounding mountains must be carried in on foot or by yak along narrow, well-worn paths through the mountains.

Before the Himalayan Trust§ built the airport in nearby Lukla in 1964, the only way in or out of Chaurikharka had been a week's walk

---

* The term Sherpa is actually the anglicized mispronunciation of the ethnic designation "Shar-wa" (literally "person from the east"). Sharwa among themselves have approximately twenty surnames, or clans (historically originating in the Tibetan province of Kham), one of which is, confusingly enough, Sharwa.

† Lhakpa can also be spelled without the h when used as a given name, which is how Lakpa Tsheri Sherpa chooses to spell his name, and thus is how he is referred to here.

‡ "Tsheri" is the Tibetan spelling. It would be "Chirring" in Nepali.

§ The Himalayan Trust is a nonprofit organization that was started by Sir Edmund Hillary. It continues to be involved in helping Sherpas better their communities through projects they themselves support but request assistance for.

through the mountains to the nearest road in Jiri. Today, it's a thirty-minute light jog to Lukla, followed by a forty-five-minute hair-raising small plane ride to Kathmandu, taking off from what The History Channel officially labeled in 2010 as the most dangerous airport in the world. Still, there are no roads.

Lakpa's parents' home, like nearly all of the structures in the village, was made of uneven stones, plucked from the terraced fields on which his family farmed. A small stand of evergreens behind the two-story building offered some semblance of shade from the afternoon sun. Inside, over a high wooden threshold, on the first floor, was a low-ceilinged windowless room, filled with sacks and baskets brimming with potatoes, turnips, cornmeal, and dried yak and dzo dung (used in place of limited wood resources for fires). Up a short wooden ladder was a single, long room with wood plank floors, lined with benches for sitting or sleeping, and shelves filled with bright copper kettles. Narrow windows with whitewashed frames and no glass let in beams of sunlight to the space. It was a good, relatively wealthy home to grow up in, by Nepali standards.

As soon as Lakpa was old enough to attend school, he began skipping it. The thick forests covering the hills along his walk to the schoolhouse in the village center provided a convenient hiding place for his frequent truancies, where in lieu of his studies he enjoyed climbing trees. Sometimes his young friends would join him, and they would build small fires to cook the potatoes they stole from nearby fields. They ate them plain, roasting them first on the glowing coals, pulling them from the fire with bare hands, laughing. He and his friends got in trouble for this, of course, but Lakpa discovered early on that he "learned more from being in nature than sitting in a classroom," as he would later say.

When he wasn't working on the family farm, Lakpa liked to spend his free time riding his uncle Dawa's horse. It was a red, useful animal. And, like all of the beasts of burden in Chaurikharka, it was allowed to roam free through the village because there are no fences. On account of this, the horse would often wander where it was not supposed to go—namely, into the forest. It was during these wanderings that Lakpa and Kili—Lakpa's older cousin by more than ten years, and Dawa's son—would be sent to retrieve it. The two boys, easily finding the red horse nibbling blithely on the green undergrowth nearby, would then ride it as fast as they dared bareback into town. It was Lakpa's first taste of speed, of which he never tired.

It was also during these early years that Lakpa and Kili's climbing careers started—on a boulder in the middle of a potato field. The large, black-gray stone, located on Uncle Dawa's farm, was only a few minutes' walk from Lakpa's family's house. One side of the boulder, gently sloping toward the ground, allowed even a child to simply walk to the top and back down again. The opposing side of the massive rock, however, formed a steep, textured wall nearly 20 feet high and required some technical climbing skills to surmount. Uncle Dawa, an experienced mountaineer and professional high-altitude worker who has been on expeditions all over the Himalaya, including Everest, bored holes into the top of the boulder with a hand drill. He placed three bolts into the rock and then promptly showed the two boys their first climbing anchor, using local hand-braided ropes. It wasn't long until all the young boys in the village were spending the dying light of each day climbing Uncle Dawa's rock, barefoot, with old retired climbing harnesses no longer seen as safe to use for Dawa's paying clients.

It was all good fun for the children, but it wasn't just for fun. Few things are for children in Nepal. Climbing is big business in the Solu-Khumbu, and nearly all of the children who started climbing on Uncle Dawa's rock knew that they too would one day work in the mountains as sherpas, climbing for their livelihood, Kili and Lakpa included.

— ~ —

Although the term *sherpa* with a lowercase *s* is typically used by mountaineers as a job description for someone who carries loads at altitude for a fee, *Sherpa* is also an ethnicity—like Arab, Anglo-Saxon, or Aztec.

Originating in the Kham region of Tibet and traditionally devout Buddhists, ancestors of the oldest Sherpa clans were eventually run out of their homelands in the thirteenth century by confrontational, catapult-wielding Mongols. And then again in the sixteenth century by a group of similarly disgruntled Muslims, finally settling down beneath the shadow of Everest in the remote Solu and Khumbu Valleys of Nepal. Immigrants continued to flow out of the mountains from the north, driven from Tibet by famine, disease, war, the usual—all of whom gradually assimilated into the Sherpa community, creating even more clans, each with its own unique culture and, oftentimes, dialect.* Nepal's most recent census in 2011 actually considers Sherpa to be a self-reported ethnicity. That is to say, any Nepali can claim to be one. The same census also notes there are approximately 102 different ethnicities within Nepal that speak about ninety-two different languages among them, not including the myriad different dialects of each language.

According to the 2011 survey, there are approximately 150,000 self-proclaimed Sherpas in Nepal who, even at this generous estimate, make up less than 1 percent of the country's total population. And despite the common use of the term *sherpa* to describe nearly everyone working as a porter or guide in the Himalaya, very few of them actually serve as porters or guides, unless, of course, they live near Everest. The desire of foreigners to come and climb the tallest mountain in the world, and their seemingly inexhaustible willingness to spend a lot of money while doing it, has become a reliable cornerstone of the Solu-Khumbu Sherpas' economy—the other being potatoes,† which are not nearly as lucrative, or deadly.

Since foreigners first started climbing in Nepal in the late nineteenth century, over 174 climbing sherpas have died while working in

---

* Dialects between Sherpa communities vary as much as 30 percent—not enough to officially count as separate languages, but enough to be thoroughly confusing.

† Potatoes, although currently the main cash crop in the Sherpa economy, are a fairly recent phenomenon in Nepal—introduced first in the nineteenth century by British travelers. Traditionally, Sherpa agriculture relied on maize, barley, buckwheat, and vegetables.

the country's mountains. At least as many sherpas have been permanently disabled by rockfalls, frostbite, and altitude-related illnesses like stroke and edema while on the job. According to a July 2013 article in *Outside* magazine, "A sherpa working above Base Camp on Everest is nearly ten times more likely to die than a commercial fisherman—the profession the Centers for Disease Control and Prevention rates as the most dangerous nonmilitary job in the United States—and more than three and a half times as likely to perish than an infantryman during the first four years of the Iraq war."

The Khumbu climbing boom, as it were, started over 100 miles to the east in Darjeeling, India, in the late 1800s, when Sherpas began migrating there to look for jobs. The first British mountaineering expeditions headed to Mount Everest in the early twentieth century—traveling through northeast India and Tibet, because Nepal was closed to foreigners until 1949—hired Sherpas to carry their things. It was to become an enduring standard for every future climbing expedition in the Himalaya. Even today.

Originally tasked with toting the enormous amount of supplies needed—or that was thought to be needed—for the early military siege–style expeditions, which tended to measure their equipment in tons rather than pounds or kilograms, let alone ounces, the Sherpas quickly proved themselves exceedingly practical, strong, and apparently more than willing to suffer horribly for what the Europeans considered a small amount of money. They carried eighty-plus-pound loads up to 18,000 feet, without complaint. They slept outside in subfreezing temperatures under boulders. Some of the women brought their babies while working, carrying loads for the foreign climbers. Their employers commended them for being "cheerful," regardless.

After a failed attempt on Everest in 1922, the British climbing legend George Mallory, who would later lose his life on the upper slopes of Mount Everest, reported to a joint meeting of the Royal Geographical Society and the Alpine Club that the greatest lesson learned from the expedition that year was that the Sherpas "far exceeded their expectations." They carried loads to 25,500 feet, he reported. Some three days in a row. Seven Sherpas also died in an avalanche on the North Col to learn this lesson. They were Everest's first recorded fatalities—the first of many more to come, for both the Sherpas and the foreigners.

Lakpa's father, Nima, who worked in the mountains during the climbing season, wanted to give his son another career option, however. And so he convinced a generous foreign client he often guided to pay for his son's education in Kathmandu. With only one year of rural schooling behind him, Lakpa abruptly found himself plucked from the mountains, put on a small, bone-rattling plane, and deposited swiftly in a boarding school surrounded by over a million people and a thick cloud of smog.

It proved to be an unstable place for the young Lakpa, in more ways than one.

⁓

Placed inconveniently near one of the world's most active fault lines, where the Indian subcontinent collides violently with Asia, Kathmandu was first razed by the movements of the earth's crust in 1253, then again in 1259, 1407, 1680, 1810, 1833, 1860, and once more in 1934. Tens of thousands died. And the next major quake will likely be worse than all of them.

The off-white haze hanging over Kathmandu is also a threat, but less sporadic. Smoke and soot, which billow up from the city's myriad brick factories, buses, cars, trucks, motorcycles, and scooters—cradled by an amphitheater of mountains—linger, even at night. People walking on the labyrinth of narrow, busy streets—flooded by, in addition to motorized vehicles, bicycles, cows, chickens, dogs, food carts, street children, and beggars—can be seen wearing surgical masks to help filter the grit of the air from their lungs. Those who don't cover up cough black phlegm.

Lakpa spent the next eight years in the city attending boarding school, where he learned to read, to write, and to like beer, cigarettes, and motorcycles. He was allowed to return to his family's farm in Chaurikharka for one week every year. He liked beer, cigarettes, and motorcycles, but not school. After failing his final exams in tenth grade, he left school for good and returned to the mountains, without any idea as to what to do next. "I had no plan," he admits. "None."

Lakpa's cousin Kili, meanwhile, had become a highly skilled climbing sherpa, working for one of Nepal's largest mountaineering outfitters, Equator Expeditions. Knowing his younger, educated cousin didn't have a career plan, he volunteered to teach Lakpa the basics of mountaineering: how to put on crampons, tie knots, and camp at altitude in the Himalaya without freezing to death, all while guiding on an "easy" nearby, nontechnical, 20,075-foot mountain rising up from the Khumbu Glacier called Lobuche East. Lakpa, as it turned out, proved to be a faster learner in the mountains than he was in the city, and he caught on quick. The only problem he encountered was on the summit, where an acute case of altitude sickness—a blinding headache that "made lights flash in my eyes," he says—nearly immobilized him. This, of course, did not dissuade him from venturing back into the mountains.

Not long after climbing Lobuche East, Kili took Lakpa to 20,305-foot Island Peak, another "trekking mountain," on which Lakpa had no difficulty and proved to be a valuable member of the expedition, namely by making the clients laugh. His infectious, broad grin never left his face the entire trip. He would often crack jokes and was caught singing happily to himself regularly—he still does. "It's what I do when I'm happy," he says.

Kili continued to hire Lakpa as an assistant on the lower peaks of the Himalaya, which in turn gave Lakpa a source of income outside of the family farm. "I climb for work, not for fun," Lakpa is quick to point out to Westerners who ask him if he enjoys mountaineering. "Climbing is not fun," he says plainly. As if it were obvious. "Climbing is hard work." This is always followed by a deep, booming, open-mouth laugh. "I do not climb for fun. Climbing is my job."

In 1998 Kili started his own mountaineering outfitter in Kathmandu called High Altitude Dreams (HAD). He sent Lakpa with a group—again as an assistant—to climb his first "technical" mountain—22,349-foot Ama Dablam, a sharp, fearsome-looking, ice-covered mountain near Mount Everest in eastern Nepal. The next year, Lakpa was sent by HAD to his first training course with the Nepal Mountaineering Association, so he could officially become certified to work at altitude in Nepal. It was a one-month course. In 2000 Lakpa was sent to another month-long tutorial to receive his "advanced" certificate. From these courses he learned, mainly, "how much I didn't actually know about mountaineering," he says. And it was at this time that he had his first opportunity to work on Everest, which he promptly declined.

Kili had offered him a job working as a high-altitude porter for an upcoming Everest expedition—the highest-elevation and highest-paying sherpa gig in the world. Lakpa could earn more than a year's wages in just two months, if he said yes. It was a lucky break in many respects, because he didn't have the level of experience typically required to work on Everest—and Lakpa, after his various safety trainings, knew this. He determined it would be too dangerous, for him and the client, so he politely turned his cousin Kili down.

Lakpa spent three more years working as an assistant on trips up shorter peaks in the Himalaya before finally agreeing to climb on Everest, contracted through High Altitude Dreams to work with the American 2003 Everest Treks 50th Anniversary Expedition Team; it was led by a thirty-nine-year-old American real estate investor from Auburn, Massachusetts, named Paul Giorgio. The trip went well, and Lakpa found himself standing on the roof of the world for the first time on Monday, May 26, 2003, at 5:57 a.m. Giorgio, an avid Boston Red Sox fan, left a black-and-white picture of New York Yankees legend Babe Ruth, "to beat the curse of the Bambino," he says (it seemed to work).* Lakpa would eventually return to this spot three more times.

It was at this moment, on Lakpa's first Everest summit, that he initially thought of the idea of flying off the top of the world's tallest mountain. In his mind it was simply a matter of practicality. *Much easier than walking down,* he thought. He had seen paragliders hovering lazily over the smog in Kathmandu Valley when he was a boy, gently gliding on the breeze, and now he decided it would be a convenient way to get off the mountain, especially considering the long, treacherous two-day descent to Base Camp ahead of him, which has actually killed more climbers on Everest than the ascent. *Much safer,* he thought.

---

* Two years earlier, Giorgio had stood on top of Everest and placed a Red Sox cap on the summit, along with an American flag for the same purpose, at a lama's suggestion. He reportedly also burned a Yankees cap with kerosene when he returned to Base Camp. The Red Sox didn't win the World Series that year, but Giorgio's 2003 gesture must have done the trick: Boston claimed the World Series title in 2004, breaking its eighty-six year drought.

III

The Learning Curve

Pokhara, Nepal,
January 2000—Approximately 2,625 Feet

"Lakeside," the man said, and kept walking. "A bus will be here soon. It's 60 rupees." Babu didn't understand the answer to his question. *Lakeside? It's a funny word,* he thought, a word he had never heard before. It sounded to him a bit like the word *lake,* which, in Sunuwar, the language spoken back in his village, means something to the equivalent of "a high place." It was 5:00 a.m., and he was standing alone in the Pokhara bus station with no idea of where he was or where to go next.

A bus to take me where? Babu wondered.

There were still only 20 rupees in his pocket. The old man he had been traveling with said good-bye to him and good luck, and then he wandered off to beg on his own.

The first rays of the morning sun began to faintly illuminate the Annapurna Massif looming to the north. Rising up over 26,000 feet, they were the tallest mountains Babu had ever seen. *Oh no,* he thought. *That's probably where Lakeside is.* It certainly looked to be the highest place nearby. And it probably wasn't going to be a cheap 60-rupee bus ride either, he figured. It would take at least a day for a bus to get there, he guessed, appraising the hazy pyramid-shaped peak in the distance.

What Babu didn't know is that Lakeside, the name for Pokhara's tourist district on the eastern shore of nearby Phewa Lake, was actually less than a mile away. He could walk there in under ten minutes. When the bus finally arrived and the attendant asked for 60 rupees to take him there, Babu was ecstatic. He still couldn't afford the ticket, but the attendant let him on anyway, appreciating his excitement. It was only a few minutes' drive, after all, and the young boy seemed to be particularly eager about it, even though he could have easily walked.

After only a few minutes on the road, Babu saw his first lake. The vast expanse of Phewa Tal came into view in pieces at first—a patch of blue between two banyan trees, blocked by buildings, flitting in between alleyways. Even with the punctuated view, Babu could tell that this new body of water was bigger than any of the mountain rivers he had ever seen, and eerily still: unmoving, flat, and over a mile across. *Wow . . . what is this?* Babu wondered. Then, glancing down a narrow street leading to the shore between two buildings, he saw a man on the water, sitting in a kayak, like the ones he had seen floating down the Sun Kosi River near his village. *This is it,* he thought.

"Stop the bus!" he yelled. "Stop! Stop! Stop!"

The sun was above the horizon now, and the valley's morning fog began to lift as Babu ran into the street. On the sidewalk, lying on the pavement not far from where he was standing, he saw a line of neon-colored whitewater kayaks, each anywhere from 6 to 9 feet long, scratched and faded from years of unapologetic rental use. Looking farther down the street in each direction, he could see even more kayak shops: their brightly colored boats sporadically lining the sidewalk off into the distance. (There are still well over a dozen of the shops in town. Pokhara is the self-proclaimed "Whitewater Capital of Nepal.") He approached the store immediately in front of him, smiling from ear to ear, excited to have finally found a place where someone, anyone, might be able to teach him how to kayak.

"Can I have a job?" he bluntly asked the man opening up the shop in front of him. "I want to learn how to kayak."

Evaluating the short, skinny frame of the boy standing in front of him, the man replied bluntly in return. "You're too small," he said with a frown. "You can't work for us."

Undeterred, Babu walked down the street to the next shop he could see with kayaks in front of it and asked the same question again.

"Do you even know how to swim?" they asked him.

"Yes!" Babu said, thinking that the skill his father taught him back in the village might just help him land his dream job. The shop owner didn't believe him, however, and asked him to leave.

At the next kayak shop he visited, they yelled at him to get out before he could even explain that he was actually willing to work in exchange for paddling lessons. The rest of the day, Babu walked from kayak shop to kayak shop, asking for work with no success. He soon began to wonder where he was going to sleep. The sun was beginning to drop, casting long shadows on the pavement. He suddenly realized how hungry he had become. He hadn't eaten all day. Finding an empty bus stop bench, Babu laid down and cradled himself for a long, cold night's sleep. Confident in the fact that he would now, after running away from home for the second time, and after having traveled more than halfway across the country, learn how to kayak. Soon.

Charley Gaillard, owner of the Ganesh Kayak Shop in Pokhara, had known Babu for nearly two years now—ever since the small boy had shown up on a bus with a big smile and started asking every kayak shop owner in town for work. Gaillard, a lanky white-haired Frenchman in his mid-fifties who had originally moved to Pokhara in 1974 to live with his Nepali wife, hadn't hired him at the time. Babu, despite his overwhelming desire to learn how to kayak, had wound up taking a job, out of necessity, as a trekking porter the first four months after he arrived in Pokhara, carrying supplies for foreign hikers in the foothills of the Annapurna region. After the trekking season ended in December, when the high mountain passes became too cold for tourists, Exodus Rafting, a Nepali-owned outfitter just down the road, took him on as a guide trainee. Gaillard knew that Babu helped clean the shop there, including maintaining the rental equipment, and that he seized every available opportunity to take one of Exodus's rental kayaks out on the lake.

"He is one of only a few Nepali kayakers I know who goes kayaking for fun," Gaillard says. "For everyone else it is work, guiding on the rivers," he explains. "There are so many good kayakers here, but they only paddle during the tourist season. They don't paddle when they're not working. And I think Babu went kayaking every chance he got."

Gaillard liked the boy and his enthusiasm for paddling, and they quickly became friends. He wasn't looking forward to telling the young man that Exodus had closed its doors while Babu had gone back to his village and that Babu was, once again, out of work. Yet here Babu was, standing in his shop in front of him with his backpack, fresh off the bus from Kathmandu, smiling as always. Completely oblivious to the fact that he would have to start over.

"You know," Gaillard said in Nepali laced with a heavy French accent. "Exodus is no more. It's finished."

Babu's smile faded. Gaillard knew that Babu had also been sleeping at the newly defunct outfitter and that his friend, along with now having no way to continue kayaking, was both unemployed and homeless. The same position Babu had been in two years earlier, when he had first gotten off the bus from Kathmandu.

What Gaillard didn't know is that while Babu had been away visiting his family, the seventeen-year-old had gotten married, which had turned out to be a surprise to Babu as well. While Babu had been in Pokhara learning how to kayak, his family had made arrangements for him to marry a frail-looking thirteen-year-old girl named Susmita Rai, who lived in a nearby village. They had sprung the good news, and the ceremony, upon his arrival. Susmita, who had been pulled out of school permanently for the occasion, had never met

Babu before the day they got married. After being handed a small bag of clothes by her parents, she walked, alone, through the hills to meet him at his parents' house, where they were quickly wed, and where she would now be expected to live and work. Babu promptly returned to Pokhara afterward, leaving behind a promise to return for his new child wife once he had earned enough money to bring her to west Nepal with him.

"Anyway, if you don't have a job," Gaillard told him casually, "maybe you can come in my place, and I can employ you. Maybe work here?" It was an offer Babu couldn't refuse.

He spent that night, and most every night for the next two years, sleeping on the wood floor behind the desk located in the back of the Ganesh Kayak Shop. It was then and remains today a small, vaguely rail-shaped establishment not more than 20 feet wide and 40 feet deep, with kayaks stacked along both walls and one large window occupying the front of the store. Near the back, on the wall behind the low wooden desk, a few faded pictures of kayakers and rafters paddling on nearby rivers like the Kali Gandaki, Seti Gandaki, and Trisuli hang in neat, evenly spaced frames. A small wooden statue of Ganesh, an elephant-headed deity that is revered in the Hindu pantheon as "the Remover of Obstacles" or "the Lord of Beginnings," and also the namesake of Gaillard's shop, sits cross-legged on the corner of the desk, looking forward blithely. Never moving.

Babu earned his keep by doing odd jobs around the shop and his home: cleaning the rental equipment, sweeping the floors, and cooking meals of dal bhat for Gaillard and his wife. Babu did this happily in exchange for a small amount of pay, a place to sleep, and the chance to use Gaillard's rental kayaks daily.

After learning some basic paddle strokes, which allowed him to move forward in a straight line and turn on the flat, unmoving water of Phewa Tal, Babu was then shown how to roll the boat right side up without having to exit the kayak, in the event it should ever flip over with him inside of it. It is a decidedly tricky maneuver for a beginner, known monosyllabically throughout the paddling community simply as a "roll." It required him to, essentially, bend his spine sideways, in the shape of a large *C,* and then attempt to knee himself as hard as possible in the head, thus flipping himself and the kayak right side up. It takes most beginning paddlers months of continual practice to gain any amount of proficiency at it. Babu was consistently rolling his kayak in the lake within a few weeks.

"He became a strong paddler very quick," Gaillard says. The only problem was Babu didn't have anyone to go kayaking with. Gaillard was a rafter, not a kayaker. And all of Babu's Nepali coworkers only went kayaking when they were guiding, safety boating for the rafts that carried paying clients. They couldn't afford to take the time to teach Babu how to paddle safely on a river, let alone take the time to repeatedly rescue him if he swam out of his boat, which is what beginning kayakers have a tendency to do. Babu needed someone to be on the river with him, teaching him one-on-one and rescuing him when he, inevitably, screwed up. There wasn't anyone, though, so for the first year of his kayaking career Babu simply paddled around in circles by himself on the lake, venturing out onto the Marshyangdi and Seti Rivers only a handful of times with Exodus's senior guides, preparing for the opportunity to work on moving whitewater, whenever it came.

Pete Astles, a clean-shaven, square-chinned, thirty-three-year-old professional whitewater kayaker from England, had just set his bag down in his hotel room in Lakeside when the phone sitting on the small bedside table next to him rang. He picked up the receiver. "There's someone here to see you, Mr. Astles," the voice of the hotel receptionist told him. The line was disconnected before he could ask who it was. Astles found this curious, considering he had just stepped off the bus from Kathmandu. As far as he knew, no one besides the eleven other international kayakers he was traveling with even knew he was there, and none of them would have asked the receptionist to call him from the lobby. They knew where his room was and would have just walked up to his door and knocked. He walked downstairs to reception, where he was greeted enthusiastically by a short, excited-looking Nepali teen with clear, shinning eyes and an ear-to-ear grin.

"You must go kayaking with me!" the young man exclaimed, quickly pumping Astles's arm with an overly firm but heartfelt hand-shake. Only after some hurried, confused discussion did Astles dis-cover that the boy's name was Babu and that his boss, their mutual friend Charley Gaillard at the Ganesh Kayak Shop, had suggested Babu go seek him out. Gaillard had known that Astles was going to be in town that month for the Himalayan Whitewater Challenge, a kayaking festival held annually in Pokhara, which Astles helped host each year through the kayaking gear company he worked for, Peak UK. Babu, armed with this knowledge, had apparently started walk-ing through town looking for foreigners with kayaks. He had seen the boats on top of the bus parked in front of Astles's hotel and figured that's probably where he was.

"He basically pestered me until I took him paddling," Astles says. Babu followed him and his friends to supper that night and listened intently to every word they said. According to Astles, "He just wanted to learn everything about kayaking that he possibly could." He couldn't help but like Babu and his infectious grin. And so he agreed to take him out on the river.

"His paddling just kept getting better and better," Astles says. "I could tell he was very, very talented right away." The professional pad-dler from the UK and his friends showed Babu how to paddle on the river on relatively easy Class II whitewater: how to move with it while sitting inside of a tippy boat approximately the size of a bathtub. How to see the different parts of the river—the waves, holes, pour-overs, sieves, and numerous other features—and how to recognize which ones were safe to interact with and which ones weren't. They had a hard time believing that Babu had swam some of the Class IV big water rapids on the Sun Kosi, "just for fun," when he was a child. They also showed him how to surf standing waves, which Babu caught on to with a flourish. "We would show him new freestyle tricks, and within a few minutes he'd have it dialed in," Astles says. It takes even expert paddlers sometimes months to master some of the complex maneuvers Babu learned, often in the same amount of time it would take most people to make a sandwich.

That next year, in 2003, Babu and his wife moved into Gaillard's home to live with him along with his wife and daughter. (Babu had fulfilled his promise to Susmita, bringing her to Pokhara two years after their marriage, though she had never before left village life and wasn't sure she wanted to.) When Astles returned to Nepal that year for the Himalayan Whitewater Challenge, he spent nearly a week paddling down Babu's home river with him—the Class III-IV Sun Kosi, a relatively advanced high-volume run—to visit Babu's family in Rampur-6.

Five years after first leaving home, Babu found himself standing on the sandy beach below his home village with a paddle in his hand and a kayak at his feet, a neoprene spray skirt dangling at his waist, a PFD on his shoulders, and a helmet on his head. It was his childhood dream come true. "My first adventure dream," as Babu puts it. But like most dreams people live to see realized, it wasn't enough. After visiting his family for a few days, Babu and Astles got back into their boats and paddled downriver, looking for new adventures.

In the years that followed, Babu and Astles ran numerous Himalayan rivers together, including the committing 82-mile Class IV+ Tamur, which drains from Kanchenjunga, the third-highest peak in the world, and the infamous Dudh Kosi: the River of Everest.

Starting at 17,500 feet from the toe of the Khumbu Glacier at the base of Mount Everest, the Dudh Kosi runs alongside the main footpath leading to Everest Base Camp, dropping over 13,000 feet in the first 50 miles with an average gradient loss of 600 feet per mile. It's a six-day, Class V-VI run, prone to massive flooding,* that didn't see its first kayak descent until 1976.

"There were some pretty stiff rapids," Astles admits. "Babu would just be like, 'Ah, possible.' We would all walk around a dangerous-looking section, and he would just run everything. Always nailed it perfectly, no worries at all." It was on this trip that Babu first saw Everest.

Gaillard points out, "Babu is not into competition." However, whenever he did choose to compete, he did well. Babu took second in the junior division at the Himalayan Whitewater Challenge in 2004. The year after, he took second place in the senior division.

Babu was quickly becoming one of the world's best kayakers, paddling the hardest, most committing whitewater in the Himalaya—and not only with Astles, but with other international whitewater heavyweights too. He befriended and boated with Gerry Moffatt, a Scotland-born, Idaho-based whitewater paddler and adventure filmmaker who was a member of the first successful expedition to paddle the legendary "Upper Gorges" of the Great Bend of the Yarlung Tsangpo in Tibet in 2002. Moffatt also was part of another expedition set up for *Men's Journal* and the Outdoor Life Network that became the first to paddle North America's "Triple Crown," three of the hardest rivers on the continent—Canada's Grand Canyon of the Stikine and Susitna, and Alaska's Alsek—in under four weeks. Babu met him when Moffatt set out to become the first person to paddle all of Nepal's major river drainages. Babu joined him on several of those expeditions. Babu also started paddling with the equally young but highly skilled American Erik Boomer, a world-class expedition kayaker and photographer who led Babu off his first 40-plus-foot waterfall on the nearby Burundi Khola River when they were both nineteen.

---

* Flooding on the Dudh Kosi and other rivers in the Himalaya is intermittently caused by a glacial lake outburst flood (GLOF), in which a glacial lake contained by continually shifting ice and moraine suddenly bursts, releasing a staggering amount of water in a matter of minutes. One on the Dudh Kosi in August 1985 had a flow of 11,000 cubic meters per second—seventeen times the average flow for that time of year. A 30-foot-high wall of water, mud, and debris swept away bridges and houses and in places even gouged out an entirely new river channel.

"Babu watched me go over the falls first," Boomer says of his first visit to Nepal in 2003 when he met Babu. "I went over the handlebars, landed upside down, but rolled up fine in the pool below. I'm sure it looked bad. Babu ran it anyway. I think he was the first Nepali to run a waterfall that big."

Babu spent what little money he earned from working with Gaillard to pay for dozens of expeditions across Nepal to northern India, oftentimes picking up odd jobs along the way to pay for gas and food. "I remember he told me about one paddling trip he took with Gerry Moffatt to northern India," Boomer recalls. "He was on his own, on his way back to Nepal, and somehow ran out of money, somewhere real high in elevation. And he had to stop for a month and chip rocks to make gravel for a road to make enough money to finish the trip."

—◆—

Abruptly, in 2006, Babu switched his career from kayaking to paragliding. The modified parachute of a paraglider (which is differentiated from a hang glider because it lacks a rigid frame) holds the pilot aloft through a series of eight precariously thin-looking support lines, which in turn are attached to a chairlike harness the pilot sits in while operating two "brake" handles dangling overhead, in order to control the descent from whatever high place he or she has leapt from. "It's a lot like kayaking," Babu says. "The air moves like water, and you have to read it the same way and anticipate what's going to happen next." The only difference is the medium you're trying to read is all around you, above and below. And you're in a chair in the sky.

"I don't know what happened," Gaillard says, reflecting on Babu's sudden switch from paddling off waterfalls to jumping off cliffs. "A few kayakers here had stopped kayaking and started flying, so maybe he thought, 'Why not?' So he tried it, and he liked it. More than kayaking, I think. So he starts paragliding, and does one day, two days, three days; and then same like kayaking. Now he's crazy about the paragliding. Starting again. New life, new sport. And he learned very quick, same as kayaking. He took a course, and now, every day he flies—too much." As it turns out, being a tandem paragliding pilot happens to pay almost double the wages of safety kayakers and whitewater guides in Nepal. "He can definitely make more money paragliding," Gaillard says.

The three-day introductory paragliding course Babu took at the lake and nearby Sarangkot was under the tutelage of Swiss pilot David Arrufat, owner of Pokhara's Blue Sky Paragliding and the head of the recently founded Association of Paragliding Pilots and Instructors (APPI). He is a 6-foot-tall "acro" (acrobatic) pilot with dark, cropped hair; a heavy, slow Swiss accent (which makes him sound perpetually tired); and a rather unique claim to fame: being the inventor of the Rhythmic SAT, an aerial paragliding maneuver that involves going into a spiral and eventually flipping end over end, in midair, repeatedly—on purpose.

"Lots of Nepalese ask me to teach them how to fly," Arrufat says of his and Babu's first meeting in Pokhara. "But they want me to give them everything for free. Babu tells me, 'I want to learn. I don't have money, but I can work.' I say, 'OK, tomorrow you start.' Many come and say, 'I want money,' or 'Give me a glider.' He's the only one to say, 'I can work.'" So Babu told Gaillard he couldn't work for the Ganesh Kayak Shop anymore and started from the bottom, cleaning and organizing gear and cooking meals for the instructors and participants at Blue Sky Paragliding in exchange for flying lessons. He was on a new adventure.

That same year, Astles took Babu mountaineering for the young Nepali's first time on 20,305-foot Island Peak, a relatively easy "trekking mountain" near Everest in eastern Nepal. It typically requires nothing more than a strong pair of legs and lungs, along with guidance from hired sherpas, to climb. Moffatt's Kathmandu-based guide company, Equator Expeditions, led and helped fund the expedition. Bad weather and Babu coming down with a severe case of altitude sickness stopped them from reaching the summit; however, the rarified air had, along with inducing a white-hot migraine, planted an audacious idea in Babu's mind: paraglide off Mount Everest.

He discussed his idea with Arrufat and Astles shortly after the expedition, while eating dal bhat together in the shade at a small restaurant by the lake after a day of flying.

"He was really kind of proud to take us to dinner and tell us his idea," Astles says. "We didn't dismiss it immediately, but we kind of looked at each other and thought in our own minds, 'That's kind of crazy.' We said, 'Oh, wow. That's an undertaking.' That was it. He kind of stunned us with this idea, I think."

Babu then asked Arrufat if it was possible to fly a paraglider from the top of Mount Everest. "It's possible," Arrufat told him. "But I think you should learn to fly a little better first."

IV

The Ultimate Descent

Darley Dale, the United Kingdom, March 2011—327 Feet

Pete Astles was sitting at his desk in his office at the Peak UK building in Darley Dale, England, checking his e-mail, when he received an unexpected phone call from Babu, asking him for a tandem kayak. And quick. "To paddle to the ocean," Babu explained excitedly over the receiver. He told Astles that he needed the boat within the month; that he had met a climbing Sherpa named Lakpa who was going to take him to the top of the world, and then jump off of it with him, and then paddle to the Bay of Bengal. That their weather window was closing, and that they were leaving for Everest Base Camp within the month. He also told Astles that Lakpa had never kayaked before and didn't know how to swim. It had been over five years since Astles and Babu had sat by the lake in Pokhara and had their first, and last, talk about Babu flying off of Everest. The idea of paddling to the ocean was completely new to Astles.

Miraculously, Astles not only believed Babu, but also agreed to help him without hesitation. He immediately dropped everything he was doing and began trolling the Internet, trying to find a boat for Babu and his new Sherpa friend who apparently couldn't swim.

"I've got contacts within the industry," Astles says. "So we quickly found a Perception that wasn't too long, I thought, and within a few hours we had a boat lined up for him." The freight company told Astles that he couldn't get anything into Nepal longer than 4 meters, since only passenger planes fly in and out of Kathmandu. "I had to rethink," Astles says. The only thing he could find to send that was less than 4 meters but still a tandem was a boat manufactured by Jackson Kayaks: the "Dynamic Duo," a 12-foot-long, eighty-pound roto-molded polyethylene craft that has an uncanny resemblance to a log and costs $1,450.

"I don't think it was ideal," Astles admits, citing the whitewater boat's exceedingly slow nature on flat water. He knew that the sections of the Ganges that Babu and Lakpa would be paddling were going to be flatter than a chapati. "But with Lakpa not knowing how to paddle or swim, it's not like they could take two singles," Astles acknowledges. So he called Babu back in Nepal and told him they'd have their boat by the time they reached the river at the end of May. How it was going to get to the river after arriving in Kathmandu, exactly, Astles wasn't quite sure.

———

After five months of flying together around Pokhara, Lakpa and Babu had eventually shared their separate dreams of flying off the top of the world with one another. After a few more weeks of shared daydreaming and several beers at the Pokhara Pizza House, they eventually decided that it would make sense for them to climb Everest together, paraglide from the top, and then paddle to the ocean. It was as simple as that. Babu's paragliding and paddling experience would make up for Lakpa's limited paragliding experience and nonexistent paddling experience, they figured; Lakpa's climbing experience would counterbalance Babu's noticeable lack of technical climbing experience. Lakpa had led inexperienced Westerners up Everest before, after all. "I trusted Babu's flying and kayaking abilities," Lakpa says. "And I trusted Lakpa to keep me safe on the mountain," Babu confirms. "So why not?" Lakpa asks. It all made sense, in theory.

They initially planned to do the expedition a few years out, giving themselves time to prepare. After all, the narrow, one- to two-week "weather window" for climbing Everest near the end of May each year was fast approaching.

The weather window is only a few days when the fierce westerly jet stream, a river of air that blasts the summit with winds often over 100 miles per hour, is moved off the summit by the oncoming monsoon from the Indian Ocean and its accompanying deluge of precipitation. Attempt to climb Everest before the weather window, and you risk getting blown off the mountain. Too late, and you're likely to get stuck on top of the world in the middle of a monsoon-scale blizzard. After hearing from some friends that two other foreign teams were going to try to fly from the summit that year, however, Babu and Lakpa decided to scrap preparedness for the chance to do it first.

The two other people attempting to fly off Everest that year were twenty-nine-year-old British adventurer and television personality Louise Falconer, better known as "Squash," and the Brazilian mountaineer and paragliding pilot Rodrigo Raineri. Squash, a pretty, short blonde with a perky, if not overtly bubbly, personality, had the self-proclaimed goal of becoming the first woman to paraglide off of Everest solo. Raineri, a strong, dark, thoughtful mountaineer, was doing it in an attempt to raise awareness of global warming and alpine water pollution, which has become a growing problem in the world of high-altitude leisure activities. He figured he would get more attention for his cause if he flew off the top of Everest. Each was named in *Outside* magazine's 2011 list of "This Year's Top 10 Everest Expeditions." And each knew that they weren't going to be the first person to paraglide off the summit. The French paragliding pilot Jean-Marc Boivin had already taken that prize in 1988. And even he wasn't the first one to fly off of Everest, or numerous other 8,000-plus-meter peaks around the world. Lakpa and Babu weren't aware of Everest's already well-established aerial stunt history, however. And if they were going to plan an Everest summit-to-sea expedition in under a month, which is exactly what they were proposing to do, it's somewhat understandable that they didn't have the time to research it extensively, or at all.

⁓

For all practical purposes, free flying in the Himalaya started (or at least was first noticed) on September 6, 1979, when twenty-eight-year-old Frenchman Jean-Marc Boivin—a talented mountaineer, skier, BASE jumper, and pilot with a gift for self-promotion—launched a hang glider from 24,934 feet off the Southwest Ridge of Pakistan's 28,251-foot K2. Known locally as Chogo Ri, "the Great Mountain," or in climbing circles as "the Savage Mountain," it's the second-highest peak in the world behind Everest. And also one of the deadliest: One out of every four climbers who has stood on the summit has died on the mountain, usually on the descent. It's also considered to be significantly more difficult to climb than Everest to begin with.

Boivin's four-month-long expedition was the biggest and most expensive in K2's history at that point. Over 1,400 porters carried more than twenty-five tons of equipment to the expedition's base camp at roughly 16,400 feet. There were ten filmmakers, press photographers, and journalists. The climbing team eventually turned down 525 feet from the summit, after attempting a new route to the top, but after returning to Camp IV, Boivin decided to descend the rest of the mountain attached to a paraglider, which the team's porters had, conveniently, carried over 8,530 vertical feet up the mountain for him. The flight back to base camp lasted thirteen minutes, and in the process, Boivin set the record for world's highest hang glider takeoff and effectively introduced the world to the novel concept of not only climbing, but jumping off 8,000-meter peaks. The K2 flight won Boivin the International Award for Valour in Sport, a prize given to him at an awards ceremony in London in February 1980.

The first person to jump off the actual summit of an 8,000-meter peak, with either a hang glider or paraglider, was French alpinist Pierre Gevaux, who launched a very early-model paraglider from the top of 26,258-foot Gasherbrum II, the world's thirteenth-highest mountain, on the border of Pakistan and China, on July 11, 1985. Only three days later, Boivin wound up launching his hang glider from the very same spot.

The paraglider design (essentially an outsize parachute) that Gevaux used on Gasherbrum II had only recently been rediscovered and popularized in Europe. It originally had been conceptualized by a NASA consultant named David Barish back in the 1960s. Barish had called his invention, designed to launch from and sail over gradual slopes in the United States, the Sail Wing (the term *paraglider* originated at NASA). Barish tested the Sail Wing himself by launching it from Mount Hunter, New York. It worked. Then nothing happened. The idea was shelved.

The Sail Wing didn't catch on until 1978, when French parachutists at Mieussy in Haute-Savoie tried launching their ram-air parachutes by running down nearby mountain slopes. Their experiments soon developed into the rather outlandish sport of parapente, an activity defined best as not quite BASE jumping, in that there was no free fall involved (hopefully), but close, in that you couldn't really control where you landed all that well. For example, as Lowell Skoog shares in his 2007 article in the *Northwest Mountaineering Journal*, "On a Wing and a Prayer," a parapente pilot nicknamed "Downwind Dave" had the misfortune of landing in a Canadian Forces rifle range after a flight from Mount Mercer in the Chilliwack Valley, British Columbia. Standing at the takeoff, his friends watched, horror-struck, as he touched down in the middle of a live-fire military zone. A few minutes later, Dave's voice crackled to life on the radio. "Downwind Dave here," he said. "I'm fine, but the soldiers are very angry." Regardless, by the early 1980s most of the major peaks in the Alps—the Aiguille Verte, Mont Blanc, the Matterhorn, and Eiger—as well as most of the major peaks in the US Pacific Northwest had all been descended by parapente.

In the same *Northwest Mountaineering Journal* article, Skoog astutely points out that the media took notice when *Climbing* magazine published a feature on parapente in April 1987. Around the same time, he also notes, *Rock & Ice* magazine, *Climbing*'s main competitor, published another. All of a sudden, people—mainly climbers—outside of the Alps knew what parapente was. And they liked it, he says. *Climbing*'s description of the activity was decidedly favorable at first: "It packs to the size of a small sleeping bag, weighs about as much as an eight millimeter rope, and is used to effortlessly descend in minutes from climbs which used to require hours or days of painful and sometimes dangerous effort . . . As skis and ice tools expanded the boundaries of alpinism to snow and ice, the parapente makes the sky the limit!" *Rock & Ice* published an article that claimed, simply, "It beats a magic carpet!" The only problem was people were getting hurt left and right doing it: crashing into cliffs, breaking both of their legs, or worse. Soon, proponents of the sport, who still considered themselves climbers first, parapente enthusiasts second, also realized that in order to do it safely, they now needed to plan their climbing trips around flying conditions. It was a tricky proposition. You could climb a mountain in a gale, but you'd be smart not to try to fly off of it in one. And it was a notable and frustrating discomfort to haul a wing up a mountain, just to carry it back down. Paragliding, it was generally decided, at least according to Skoog, was something you did as an end in itself, not a part of regular, ideally safety-oriented, mountaineering.

In a 1992 interview in *Rock & Ice*, Mark Twight, a respected climber and paragliding pilot in the Pacific Northwest, was blunt about it. "It's useless for climbing," he said. "It's the most seductive thing to say, 'Oh man, I'm so wasted, I'll just fly down.' But the conditions are rarely right. I never got over my fear. I'd be on top, and I'd throw up. The most fun for me was packing my parachute after I landed—'Wow, I lived.'"

Naturally, this didn't stop people from doing it, and the attention of those looking to fly off the world's tallest mountains inevitably turned to Everest. In the fall of 1986, US pilots Steve McKinney and Larry Tudor became the first to attempt to launch themselves off the slopes of Everest. And from the outset, flying off of the peak proved to be as much a logistical challenge as a physical one. The idea was to take hang gliders off the West Ridge, on the Tibetan side of the mountain. Chinese customs became suspicious of the odd-looking contraptions, however, and impounded them upon McKinney and Tudor's arrival into the country. Their friend and expedition mate Craig Colonica, a 6-foot-3, 240-pound rock and ice climber from Tahoe, California, requested their release. "Craig went ballistic," Tudor later reported to *Cross Country* magazine. "His eyes turned blood red like a deer in your headlights. He grabbed the customs guy, yanked him over the counter and with his face inches away told the interpreter, 'You tell this guy these are our gliders, we paid for them, we are here with permission from his government and if he doesn't give us them to us right now I'm going to twist his head from his skinny little neck.'"

A week later, they were in Base Camp with perfect weather. Unfortunately, the gliders, which were now out of quarantine and in transit, took a month to arrive. "We missed our window," wrote Tudor. "We had problems with jet stream winds that arrive with winter . . . The winds forced us off the mountain. I spent three days and four nights in a tent on the west ridge at 22,000 feet waiting for the winds to back off. Bob Carter, another member of the expedition, spent the next night before retreating. You haven't lived till you have been in a nylon tent in 100 mph winds." Tudor added, "[Eventually] we got one of the gliders to the top of the West Ridge. But it was too late. The jet stream winds had descended on the mountains and the expedition was out of money and wondering how we were going to get out of the country." McKinney wound up launching his glider from just over 600 feet up the West Ridge from their camp. "To appease the sponsors," Tudor explained. "He also made a very spectacular out-of-control flight to a wicked crash on the glacial moraine at base camp."

After launching off Gasherbrum II and narrowly missing the opportunity to become the first person to fly off the summit of an 8,000-meter peak behind Gevaux, Boivin achieved the first free flight from the top of Mount Everest on September 26, 1988, switching out his trusty hang glider for one of the new, relatively lightweight paragliders. Boivin reached the summit at 2:30 p.m. along with four other European climbers and two sherpas. It took them ninety minutes to prepare Boivin's wing for takeoff. The wind was reportedly gusty, blowing at up to 40 miles per hour; however, Boivin successfully managed to launch from the summit, after running 60 feet down the 40-degree summit slope. "I was tired when I reached the top," Boivin said shortly after the flight in an interview with *Backpacker* magazine. "Because I'd broken much of the trail, and to run at this altitude was quite hard." It was an understatement, at best. Most climbers on Everest report having a hard time walking, let alone sprinting through knee-deep snow on the top. Boivin safely, if not abruptly, glided down to Camp II at 19,356 feet, descending over 9,840 feet in under twelve minutes, dropping approximately 15 feet per second. With only a quarter of the air pressure there is at sea level, paragliding off the summit of Everest proved to be more like falling, just at a more survivable rate.

Vol bivouac, flying and camping through the mountains at lower altitudes, offered adventurous pilots a way to experience flying in the mountains without adding the dangers and additional costs of technical climbing and launching their wings at altitude. Because of this, vol bivouac soon became significantly more popular than launching off technical peaks, both in Europe and in the Himalaya. Still, occasionally people ventured high into the mountains to fly.

In 1990 seventeen-year-old Bertrand "Zebulon" Roche was a passenger on a successful tandem paragliding flight with his father, Jean-Noël Roche, from Everest's 8,000-meter South Col, and evidently he got hooked. He went back in 2001 to launch a tandem wing with his wife, Claire, on May 21, bagging the first-ever tandem paragliding descent off Everest's summit. Before that they had paraglided off five of the other Seven Summits, the tallest points on each continent (intentionally excluding Australia's 7,310-foot Mount Kosciuszko because it had apparently lost continent status amongst the French).* The pair, without question, had remarkable luck.

About the summit, Claire reported after the flight: "It was 8 am. The view was breathtaking. Not a cloud, the wind was between 30 to 40km/h." After taking summit photos the pair found a spot about 30 feet below the top. Claire wrote: "We took off our oxygen masks and prepared the wing. These tasks, which were so easy below, were very trying up there. It took an hour to get ready. Then, sat one on top of the other, on the edge of the mountain, Zeb put the sail up and very quickly the wind took us to that mythical place. For a few minutes, we were birds. The countryside flashed by. The conditions weren't as calm as they seemed, the west wind changed our flight path. Above the North Col, the wing started to flap violently, reminding Zeb of competition flights. We were distancing ourselves from anything which could cause turbulence. At 10:22 a.m. we set down gently on the Rongbuk glacier, just above 6,400 metres."

The Dutch pair that tried to repeat the feat in 2002 weren't so lucky. The wing sherpas had carried for them to Camp III disappeared when they were blasted by winds. The camp was "torn apart" and the glider "flew off on its own, still in its bag," the final report read.

In 1998 Russian climber Elvira Nasonova had also tried to launch a tandem paraglider from above the Khumbu Icefall on the mountain while climbing, but she crashed horribly. Reports from the day read,

---

* The highest peaks on each of the seven continents, also known as the Seven Summits, are Everest, 29,035 feet (Asia); Aconcagua, 22,834 feet (South America); McKinley (aka. Denali), 20,320 feet (North America); Kilimanjaro, 19,340 feet (Africa); Elbrus, 18,510 feet (Europe); Vinson Massif, 16,067 feet (Antarctica); and Kosciuszko, 7,310 feet (Australia). Kosciuszko's status as highest point in Australia is up for some debate. Many have argued that the highest point in Oceania, the group of lands that includes Australia and is technically part of the same continent, is not Kosciuszko but rather the 16,535-foot Carstensz Pyramid in the Indonesian province of Irian Barat.

"The start was unsuccessful. In the moment they took off from the rock a gust got up. The sportsmen were knocked against the rock, the glider soared upward and Elvira and her instructor fell down on the glacier from about 50m." The instructor escaped unscathed, but Nasonova spent three days lying injured on the glacier before she was eventually rescued by helicopter. She survived. Barely.

—— ~

In March 2011 Squash Falconer and Rodrigo Raineri were poised to be the next paragliding pilots to fly from the summit of Everest, comfortably backed by corporate sponsorships and the resulting media attention. Lakpa and Babu had just decided to beat Falconer and Raineri to it, though, over several bottles of Carlsburg beer and dal bhat at the Pokhara Pizza House, even though they had no plan, or money for that matter, to do it. They didn't have any corporate sponsors. They didn't even have the basic gear they would need to complete the expedition. Neither of them actually owned a tandem wing capable of flying off Everest, and they still had no boat they could paddle together to the ocean, even if they did manage to find an ultralight wing and, somehow, climb and fly off the top of Everest with it.

"Anything is possible," Babu told Lakpa. They agreed then that Lakpa would handle the logistics of the climbing portion of the trip and that Babu would sort out the particulars for the descent to the sea. Each of them was to be responsible for his own area of expertise: Lakpa, on the mountain, Babu, in the air and on the water. They would leave within the month, in order to make the trek to Everest Base Camp and start acclimatizing to the high altitude before either Falconer or Raineri could fly off the mountain, and, even more likely, before the spring weather window closed. They also decided, offhandedly, that they were going to film the expedition. Neither of them owned a camera.

They needed help, and quick.

Not long after Lakpa and Babu's impromptu expedition meeting at the Pokhara Pizza House, David Arrufat was woken up by the sound of loud knocking on his front door. It was 1:00 a.m., and Babu was "full of beer," Arrufat says. "He tells me, 'Hey! Let's go drink! Tomorrow, we go to Everest!'" It proved to be not the most effective way to approach a potential expedition sponsor. Arrufat, annoyed at being awoken at such an obtuse hour, told his friend/employee that he couldn't help pay for their trip, but that he could use his contacts in the paragliding world to help order them a new tandem wing, which would cost nearly $4,000. He also promised to help them in whatever way he could outside of a financial contribution. Babu then asked Gaillard, his old boss at Ganesh Kayak Shop, to help pay for the expedition.

"I gave him a few hundred dollars," Gaillard recalls. "I don't remember exactly how much, but it wasn't much. Babu offered to put the Ganesh Kayak Shop logo on the wing they were going to use, but I told him, 'No, save that for a bigger sponsor.'"

Babu's friends Kelly and Nim Magar, co-owners of Paddle Nepal, an outfitter across the street from Gaillard's shop that also assisted in hosting the annual Himalayan Whitewater Challenge, wound up being one of the most generous sponsors. They agreed to have two members of their staff, who were also friends of Babu, pick up the tandem boat that was due to arrive in Kathmandu and transport it to the confluence of the Dudh Kosi and the Sun Kosi to meet Babu and Lakpa there, after they had flown off Everest and across the mountains. The staff would be unpaid for the trip, but being friends with Babu, they volunteered anyway.

"It must have been at least four years earlier when Babu first told me about his idea to fly off Everest," recalls Nim, a stocky, compact Nepali with short black hair. "He went up to Island Peak with Pete Astles and got altitude sickness, I remember. He got sick and had to go back. So Kelly and I kind of said, 'No way, Babu. You don't do well in the mountains.' And I always just kind of brushed it off, like, 'I don't think this is such a good idea, Babu.' But he just wanted to go for it. And then he didn't really talk about it much. The plan kind of fizzled for a few years. Then I was shocked—just a few weeks before they actually went out to start, when he came into the office and was just raring to go. He had just met Lakpa. He was like, 'Bai, it's happening. We need your support.' I couldn't believe it. After so many years." The Magars also agreed to send one of their rafts and two of their staff to help set safety on the whitewater portion of the expedition, paddling with Babu and Lakpa from the confluence of the Dudh Kosi and the Sun Kosi down to Chatra, near the Indian border.

"When Babu first approached us to support the river part of the trip for him," Kelly, Nim's friendly, petite, blonde, and significantly taller American expat wife, says, "Nim and Sanchos and Song, the three brothers [and owners] of Paddle Nepal, discussed it. As much as we wanted to help them right through to the ocean, Paddle Nepal decided we would do our best to deliver the boat and keep them safe through the big rapids until they got to the Indian border, but it was a little too risky for us to send our crew outside of the country. Not for river reasons, but because of politics and banditry. We couldn't expect our crew to do that."

After calling Astles in the United Kingdom, Babu theoretically had a boat lined up, and thanks to his friends in Pokhara, he had a way to get it to the river, but he still had no wing to fly off the mountain with. Both Lakpa and Arrufat claim that they were the ones who purchased the custom-made, ultralight "Everest Wing" eventually used on the expedition. What's certain is that Arrufat was the one who placed the call that got French paragliding manufacturer Niviuk to hastily make the wing and, miraculously, ship it to Nepal in under a month.

"It is not allowed to ship a glider to Nepal," Arrufat says, citing the country's nearly 200 percent import tax. "We needed to get the glider here fast. And it needed to be light. And the company had to make it. Nobody trusted us—they say, 'No, we cannot give them glider like this.' They want proof. Everybody wanted proof. Nobody believed. No proof. They have to go by feeling." It proved to be a lot of feeling to ask. Niviuk eventually shipped the wing to Arrufat for full price. He was then able to avoid Nepali customs by having one of his friends fly over with it on a commercial flight from Malaysia, but by the time it arrived, Lakpa and Babu had already departed for Everest.

Lakpa wasn't having much luck procuring major support for the last minute-expedition either. When he asked his cousin Kili if HAD would sponsor the trip, he was politely told no, but that he could be excused from work to go if he could get the funds and logistical support put together on his own. "He told me that he wanted to climb Everest with Babu and fly down from the summit," Kili says. "I didn't feel comfortable with it at the time. I didn't tell him he couldn't do it, because I wasn't sure how the adventure would go, so I just told him, 'OK. You can go.'" Lakpa would have to find another way to pay for him and Babu to get to the top of Everest, and he knew that wasn't going to be cheap.

A typical guided Everest expedition costs—minimum—$30,000 per person. Most Western guiding companies charge $65,000. A private expedition like Babu and Lakpa's, without the backing of a guide service and the cost break given to large commercial groups, could run as much as $100,000 per person. Fortunately, for Lakpa at least, he didn't have to pay for his own climbing permit because he was a sherpa. Issued by the Nepalese government, climbing permits for non-sherpas cost $70,000 for a party of seven, or $25,000 for an individual climber. At Base Camp, all the teams combine resources to pay for the camp doctor and to pay sherpas, referred to as "the Icefall Doctors," to set the fixed ropes, so that the equipment that everyone uses to traverse the Khumbu Icefall at the base of the mountain is in place. Then there's gear, and getting to Base Camp, which is pretty consistent, price-wise, across the board. For instance, oxygen costs $500 a bottle, and climbers typically bring six bottles each. Yaks to transport gear to Base Camp run around $150 each, per day.

So Lakpa sold some of the land he had purchased after years of working as a high-altitude climbing sherpa to fund the trip. The land was in Bandipur, just to the east of Kathmandu. He had intended to eventually start another farm there, but instead sold it for approximately $20,000. It was going to have to be enough to get him, Babu, and whomever else he could find to help them, to the top of the world. He felt comforted by the fact that his friend Babu would have to worry about getting them back down.

Predictably, Lakpa's wife, Yanjee, was not pleased. After Lakpa told her that he was selling the land and spending the money to fund an expedition to jump off of Everest with Babu, someone she had never met before, she broke into tears. "I begged him not to go," she says. "I begged him. But he went anyway." She was afraid that she would have to raise their then four-year-old son, Mingma Tashi, alone if Lakpa didn't come back alive. And she knew there was a fairly good chance of that. It was dangerous enough to just climb in the Himalaya. After all, according to the Himalayan Database, 1.2 percent of climbing sherpas had already died while working in the mountains of Nepal. That number may seem small; however, as Grayson Schafer notes in his 2013 article for *Outside* magazine, "Disposable Man," "There's no other service industry in the world that so frequently kills and maims its workers for the benefit of paying clients." Commercial fishermen— the profession the Centers for Disease Control and Prevention rates as the most dangerous nonmilitary job in the United States—are ten times less likely to die on the job than a sherpa. And none of them had ever tried to actually fly off one of the mountains they were climbing. After shaky responses from both Kili and his wife, Lakpa dealt with telling the rest of his relatives about the trip by getting them "slightly drunk" first, he says.

San Francisco, California,
March 2011—Approximately 200 Feet

Kimberly Phinney had known Babu for less than a month when he called her unexpectedly at her home, just north of San Francisco, California, asking her if she could help fund his and Lakpa's upcoming Everest expedition. "We're going for sure," Babu told her. "But we have no sponsors. Can you?" Phinney, a short, petite, twenty-eight-year-old West Coast fashion designer and paragliding pilot with long, dark brown hair, ear gauges, and an owl tattoo on her left shoulder, had just returned from Nepal a week earlier after a two-month paragliding trip to Pokhara. She had lost her wallet and all of her trip cash on her third day in the country, after taking it out to leave an offering at a temple and then accidentally leaving it behind. She had spent her first month in Nepal living on a shoestring budget, borrowing money from friends, and trying to find people to fly with.

"I wanted to bivouac," Phinney says. "Hiking and flying, being free. I wanted to be surrounded by the Nepali people eating in the huts, as I remembered from my previous travels to Nepal. I searched around trying to get one of the many pilots there to be daring enough to venture off and explore some of the more remote hike-up takeoffs I had heard about." But she found no one willing to go with her, unless she was willing to pay them to take her. Then she met Babu.

"I saw a group clustered around Babu asking questions," Phinney says, referring the first time she met the young Nepali, instructing a group of European pilots at a remote launch site north of Pokhara, at the base of the Annapurnas, preparing to take off for an hour-long cross-country flight back to Phewa Tal. "The tricky thing in Nepal is there are very few good landing zones," Phinney says. "If you're up high, it's all groovy, but if you do get low, you can be locked in-between two rather large mountains." Babu, apparently, was having a difficult time communicating this in his second language, English, to a group of Europeans who also didn't speak English as their primary language. "I heard Babu repeating his words to the group, so I went over and helped out a bit, giving a more detailed English explanation of what he was saying," Phinney says. "He looked relieved and grateful."

When the flying was over that day and everyone had landed back at the lake—or had been picked up somewhere between the launch site and the lake, if they hadn't quite made it—Babu invited Phinney to go flying with him and the rest of the Blue Sky Paragliding crew—for free, he said, if she was willing to continue helping with instructing in English. "My dream finally came true," Phinney says. "I was hiking, flying, and camping out, helping the guys cook the food, drinking water from the yak huts with the porters as I carried all of my own gear. A strong friendship was formed."

Babu told Phinney, whom he and the other Nepalis had now taken to calling "Ruppy," after a local bird that has a tendency to fly straight at the ground (not a good thing if you're a paraglider), how he wanted to climb and fly off the summit of Mount Everest. "And to make it different and more interesting," Phinney says, "he told me he would then kayak to the sea. After watching him fly the past few weeks, I believed he could do anything. He told me they had no sponsor, but he didn't care. They would do it anyway." Phinney told him he deserved sponsorship if he was going to attempt something as audacious as that. "At least a free glider," she said, and then told him that she would be happy to help him with the process, if he was interested. Not long after that conversation together in the hills outside of Pokhara, she got the call from Babu, asking for help.

Phinney, who had never actually worked as a publicist before, told him, somewhat accurately, "For big sponsorships, you need a website, GPS tracker, communication equipment, and good media coverage." Babu told her that they didn't have time for any of that. They were leaving in less than a month. "So I agreed to help from my own pocket with what I could," Phinney says. "And that I would supply him with the GPS and technical side of things, and teach him how to set it up proper for a sponsor." So she wired $6,000 to Babu in Kathmandu and put a SPOT brand GPS tracker* and solar chargers in a box and mailed it to Nepal. She then created a SPOT account on Babu and Lakpa's behalf, so their movements could be tracked by followers online. "I posted it everywhere," Phinney says. "I asked him who else was helping him, so I could put their names on the GPS website, but the list was short, only a few friends' names." And all of them were just donating equipment. "I had no idea how he would pull this off with so little," Phinney admits. "But I had faith that if he thought he could do it, he would. The Nepali people are amazingly tough."

Phinney then hastily built a website with the URL theultimate-descent.com, complete with a blog for Babu and Lakpa, and demanded that they call her at least once a week to give her updates. She conferred with Babu and Lakpa together on Skype and put together a mission statement for them, partly based on what they told her, and partly on what she wanted them to say. She then posted it on the homepage of their new website:

Our vision is not only to be the first, but for us to be the First All NEPALI Expedition of this kind. We wish to support all Nepalese people in setting new records especially here in our home country. We have watched year after year as other nationalists come to Nepal and the Everest Region to set or attempt to set world records, and first ascents. This time we set out with an all Nepali team in hopes of putting the Nepalese people in this record breaking category. We also wish to contribute towards making this years Visit Nepal 2011 a success, we intend to promote adventure activities such as para-gliding, river sports, and cycling, through out Nepal.

---

* A SPOT Messenger is a handheld GPS unit that automatically relays the device's coordinates via e-mail or text message to anyone signed up to "follow" it. It also provides a link to the device's location on Google Maps, and it is capable of sending a distress signal to the GEOS Rescue Coordination Center. In Babu and Lakpa's case, the device would allow Phinney to track their progress from San Francisco.

As a way of giving back, we would also like to setup a scholarship fund and give physical or material support to schools in our more remote regions. It is our understanding that their are many schools here that are in need of educational material and other basic facilities. We intend to facilitate a way to make sure educational materials are made available to the children free of charge and help with the development of drinking water and toilet facilities. Our team feels that helping them physically/ financially just this year will not have the desired impact we are hoping for. We intend to follow up next year to further help develop these schools and perhaps make a small impact on wiping out illiteracy. Please stay turned to for more info as we continue to put this part of the dream into action.

Of course, they had no money, or even potential sponsors with the money to set up a scholarship fund. Then, with their boat and wing, GPS, and most of the other donated equipment they would need for the expedition still in transit, and no actual backing from the Nepali government, they embarked for Everest.

V

Peak XV

Tethys Sea, Cretaceous Period—Approximately
8,000 Feet below Sea Level

Around 120 million years ago, the Indian landmass did something drastic: It broke free of the Mesozoic continent of Gondwana* and began drifting northward at the rate of just over 6 inches per year, an impressive clip for a continent, considering most move, on average, less than an inch. Eventually, 75 million years later—a short, arm-flailing sprint in geological time—the Indian subcontinent ran headlong into the submerged edge of its larger neighbor, Eurasia. The impact zone was 1,500 miles wide. The denser ocean floor north of India, which was primarily made of basalt, dropped into the earth's mantle and disappeared, literally melting beneath a line of now-extinct volcanoes. The comparatively lighter sedimentary rocks of present-day India and Tibet (limestone, shale, sandstone), formed millions of years earlier on the bottom of the ancient Tethys Sea,† were thrust skyward, having no other place to go.

---

* Gondwana, also called Gondwanaland, was an ancient supercontinent that incorporated present-day South America, Africa, Arabia, Madagascar, India, Australia, and Antarctica. It was fully assembled some 600 million years ago by Late Precambrian time, and the first stage of its breakup began in the Early Jurassic period, about 180 million years ago.

† The Tethys Sea was a tropical body of salt water that separated the supercontinent of Laurasia in the north from Gondwana in the south during much of the Mesozoic Era (251 to 65.5 million years ago).

The process, which geologists refer to somewhat blandly nowadays as orogeny, created the youngest and highest-elevation mountains on the planet: the Himalaya (*Himā*, snow; *alāya*, abode). Home to the world's largest subpolar glacial systems and deepest land gorges, the "abode of snow" is also the source of three of the world's greatest river systems—the Indus, the Ganges, and the Brahmaputra. One-sixth of the world's population lives within its watershed. Averaging 6,000 meters (19,685 feet) along its northern rampart, the Himalaya also host all fourteen of the world's 8,000-meter (26,247 foot) peaks. Thirty are over 25,000 feet tall.

For perspective: The highest mountain in the Western Hemisphere, Argentina's Aconcagua (22,841 feet), wouldn't even make the top two hundred in the Himalaya. Most of the smaller peaks in the range are significantly higher than the tallest in Europe. And they're still growing. India, although noticeably slowed by its now forty-five-million-year-long continental train wreck with Asia, is still persistently moving north nearly 2 inches each year, lifting the entire mountain range about 1 centimeter every 365 days. All of it, even the summit of Mount Everest at 29,035 feet*—the highest point of elevation in the Himalaya, and thus, the world—was once at the bottom of the ocean. And after another few million years, it will return to it: one grain of silt at a time, flowing steadily out of the glaciers down the great, winding rivers of the Himalaya back to the sea. The world's tallest mountains, eventually grinding themselves down to rolling hills, like the now ancient Appalachians in the eastern United States. To say where one truly ends and the other begins is more a question of time than space or distance. And that's a much trickier thing to define.

———

* Although Mount Everest currently holds the record for being the world's highest mountain at 29,035 feet, the ninth-highest mountain, Nanga Parbat (26,660 feet), at the far western end of the Himalaya, is the fastest rising and may one day stand taller.

In 1849 field surveyors in northern India working for Britain's Great Trigonomical Survey, which had been assigned the rather daunting task of mapping, in excruciating detail, the entire Indian subcontinent for the crown, took measurements of a small speck of a mountaintop jutting up from deep within the then-forbidden kingdom of Nepal using a 24-inch theodolite. The mountain, pragmatically given the name Himalaya Peak XV, was over 100 miles away, situated at roughly 87 degrees east and 28 degrees north on the remote northeastern border of Nepal and Tibet. Due to the distance, other mountains in the foreground appeared much larger, so no special attention had been given to it at the time. Peak XV was obviously enormous, but so was everything else the surveyors were measuring. They were mapping the Himalaya, after all. The measurements sat in a folder collecting dust in Calcutta for three years until, in 1852, a mathematician named Radhanath Sikhdar finally did the math—and amazingly well. He took into account such factors as the curvature of the earth, atmospheric refraction, and plumb-line deflection (the sheer mass of a mountain creating enough gravitational pull to move a plumb line ever so slightly, thus altering measurements). Sikhdar put the summit of Peak XV at a neat and remarkably exact 29,002 feet.* It was, without a doubt, the highest point of elevation on earth. And nobody outside of Nepal or Tibet had even known it was there. The world's highest point had been hiding in plain sight for millennia.

In 1865 Sir Andrew Waugh, India's surveyor general, decided to rename the peak Mount Everest in honor of his predecessor, Sir George Everest, an intense, bearded man with sand-colored hair and a passion for accuracy that drove him on several occasions to be diagnosed as mentally ill. At first glance this would seem curious, since official policy at the time encouraged the retention of local or ancient names, which "Everest" (pronounced EEV-er-est by the family) was decidedly not. With both Nepal and Tibet being closed to foreigners at

---

* The current height of Mount Everest, calculated with lasers and Doppler satellite transmissions, is generally agreed to be 29,035 feet.

the time, however, Waugh had no way to actually ask the local Nepalis or Tibetans what they happened to call the peak, even if they did have a perfectly good name for it. And they did—two, actually. Nepalis to the south referred to the mountain as Deva-dhunga, "seat of God."* Tibetans on the north side of the mountain had been calling it Jomo-langma for centuries, named after the goddess believed to dwell there: Miyolangsangma or Jomo Miyolangsangma, whose full name means something to the equivalent of "the immovable goddess mother of good bulls." And even that has been quite regularly mistranslated, even today. In a 2013 essay written for National Geographic Books' *The Call of Everest,* Edwin Bernbaum, director of the Sacred Mountains Program of the Mountain Institute,† points out:

> *Almost every book on Everest mistranslates the Tibetan name as 'goddess mother of the universe,' based on an assumption that the Tibetan and Sherpa people who live near its base must revere the highest peak in the world as the sacred abode of a supremely impor-tant deity. But the persistent use of this translation reflects the great importance that outsiders, rather than the local Tibetans and Sher-pas, place on Everest.*

As it turns out, in Tibetan Buddhism, there isn't a goddess mother of the universe, or the world for that matter. "The idea of such a goddess doesn't fit in a religion that doesn't believe in a monothe-istic supreme creator," Bernbaum observes. He goes on to point out

---

* Today, the official Nepali designation for Mt. Everest is Sagarmatha, "goddess of the sky." The name was rarely, if ever, used before 1960. At that time there was a border dispute with China, and Nepal's prime minister, B. P. Koirala, believed it would help Nepal assert its claim to the southern side of Everest if there were a widely recognized Nepali name for it. He chose Sagarmatha at the suggestion of his advisors, and the national park that encompasses the Nepali side of the mountain still bears the name.

† Founded in 1972, the Mountain Institute is a nonprofit organization headquartered in Washington, DC, with offices in West Virginia, Nepal, and Peru (home to the world's oldest, tallest, and longest mountain ranges, respectively). It is committed to economic development in the mountains, conser-vation of mountain environments, and support for mountain cultures.

that Jomo Miyolangsangma is actually a "relatively minor goddess." Regardless, the mountain is still called Everest today.

In 1911, as Everest continued to slowly rise up from its ancient seabed, shrouded in obscurity, it suddenly became the center of the outside world's attention, at least in regard to terrestrial conquest. Shortly after, a small group of Norwegians under the command of a man named Roald Amundsen, and then another, more ill-fated British group lead by Robert Falcon Scott, stood, shivering, on the South Pole. It was the most sought-after point to stand on the globe at the time, given that the North Pole had been stood and shivered on a few years previously by an equally cold and courageous group of Americans.˙ The quest to put a human being smack-dab in the middle of each of the earth's two polar regions, alive, had taken some three hundred years and much suffering and death by people from many nations. Standing on the top and bottom of the planet, as far as latitude and longitude were concerned, had been a great and obvious goal for humankind—it was the closest thing to the ends of the earth we could find, after having discovered that we were, in fact, living on a globe. And like any great, seemingly impossible goal, once it was proven possible and then finally accomplished, it left a huge, cavernous, anticlimactic hole—filled immediately with the same question such holes are always filled with: What's next?

The answer was to be Everest: the next logical end-of-the-earth. Not long after Amundsen's successful expedition to the southernmost point on the planet, the mountain quickly became known as "the third pole," and a good number of people (mainly British) decided it would

---

* There's some debate over which American expedition, exactly, reached the North Pole first. Robert E. Peary sent word from Indian Harbour, Labrador, in April 1909, that he and his companions had reached the pole first. The news was printed on the front page of the *New York Times* on September 7. A week prior, however, the *New York Herald* had printed a front-page headline of its own, stating that Dr. Frederick A. Cook, an American explorer who, after having spent more than a year wandering in the Arctic, was given up for dead, had returned and claimed to have reached the pole in April 1908—a full year before Peary. The argument is still technically up for debate. Neither claim has been either proved or disproved, even after a full reexamination of both expeditions' records, which was commissioned by the National Geographic Society in 1988.

be a smashing idea to put a person on top of it, despite the fact that the two countries the mountain straddled, Nepal and Tibet, were unquestionably and unapologetically closed to outsiders. This new goal would take over forty years to accomplish—more than a century since it was quantified as the tallest point on earth. Likewise, it would turn out to require much suffering and death.

Several British teams rapidly made plans to sneak into both Nepal and Tibet to do reconnaissance for a potential peak-bagging mission. In 1913 a twenty-three-year-old English army captain named John Noel, who would later become one of Everest's most famous early photographers, actually took it upon himself to dress up like "a Mohammedan from India," darkening his skin and donning a black wig to better blend in with the Tibetans, and managed to sneak through the border. He got within 40 miles of Everest before being turned around and chased out of the country by the local authorities, who were still upset about the last Briton who had entered their country, nine years earlier: Francis Younghusband. Lieutenant Colonel Younghusband had entered the peaceful Buddhist country—which consciously chooses not to support an army—with ten thousand soldiers on what was supposed to be a "diplomatic" mission; he spent nearly nine months marching to Lhasa, killing somewhere around five thousand Tibetans en route and sending the Dalai Lama fleeing for his life to Mongolia. Upon returning to England, Younghusband was knighted and made director of the Royal Geographical Society.

The same year Noel snuck into Tibet to catch a glimpse of Everest, another man named Cecil Rawling boldly drafted official plans for an Everest reconnaissance, with the support of the Royal Geographical Society, which was scheduled to take place the following year. Remarkably, the India Office did not straight-out reject the proposal, even though it recommended blatantly illegal actions—namely, entering a neighboring country without permission. But it also had not approved any of the plans by June 28, 1914, when all hell broke loose in Europe. A young Bosnian nationalist in Sarajevo named Gavrilo Princip shot and killed Archduke Franz Ferdinand, heir to the Austro-Hungarian throne, and five weeks later, the entire continent was at war. No one gave much thought to Everest at all for four horrific years.

The First World War presented a new and much more immediate set of challenges to the Western world, but also helped to shape the military siege–style tactics that are still, more often than not, used when climbing on Everest or other high-altitude peaks around the world. Not entirely unlike the trench warfare strategies developed in Europe, the goal was not a quick, clean victory but a sure one, even if it was excruciatingly slow and costly. It consisted of setting up a well-stocked base camp (complete with leather furniture and full libraries during some of the earlier Everest expeditions) and then launching several repeated "assaults" on the mountain, each time gaining slightly more ground and elevation, and then setting up a new, slightly higher camp from which to launch the next assault. It was a style of climbing that required a huge amount of manpower, time, money, and, again like war, human sacrifice.

Something being named the "world's tallest" seems, on the surface, to be a fairly straightforward proposition, particularly in the case of mountains. It's not. The summit of Everest, for example, while technically the highest point of elevation on the planet at 29,035 feet above sea level, isn't actually on top of the world's tallest mountain. The summit of Mauna Kea, the highest point on the island of Hawaii at 13,796 feet above sea level, is. Rising nearly 33,500 feet from the bottom of the Pacific Ocean, only the top third of the massive shield volcano-turned-tropical-paradise is visible above water. If you were to place Mauna Kea and Mount Everest side by side on a level plane, Mauna Kea would be over 18,000 feet taller than Everest, which sits high up on the Tibetan Plateau, its base starting from anywhere between 17,100 feet when measured on the Tibetan side of the mountain to 13,800 feet when measured on the Nepal side, giving Everest a total height from top to bottom of somewhere between 12,000 to 15,300 vertical feet. Alaska's 20,322-foot Mt. McKinley (Denali) would also be taller than Everest if set next to it, rising some 18,000 feet from its approximately 2,000-foot base on the tundra of North America.

From a more cosmic perspective—let's say, looking down at earth from the moon—there are four mountains other than Everest that would appear taller from space (if you could actually see them from such a distance, which you can't).* This is on account of the earth not being perfectly round. The planet, along with its atmosphere and oceans, actually bulges 26.5 miles outward at the equator. Ecuador's 20,565-foot Chimborazo, the tallest among these bulging peaks, sits closest to the equator and thus sticks nearly 1.5 miles farther out from earth's center than Everest. If you were going to put a hat on top of the world, it would be on Chimborazo.

The truth is there is no real beginning to any mountain—and even the ends of them are maddeningly elusive.

—◆—

On December 20, 1920, news reached London that the Dalai Lama had agreed to allow a group of Britons to approach Mount Everest through Tibet. With official approval finally in hand, it took a year for the Royal Geographical Society to decide what they were going to do with it. They had been sending "pundits," a corps of trained "Tibetan-looking Indians," into both Tibet and Nepal to secretly map the countries for the British Empire since the 1860s. The pundits calculated distance by counting their own steps, using a Tibetan rosary as an abacus, and altitudes by timing the boiling point of water. They hid their field notes in prayer wheels they carried, and their thermometers in their staffs. Now they had permission to do it.

---

* The four mountains whose summits are even farther away from earth's center than Everest (3,965.8 miles from the planet's core), are Tanzania's 19,341-foot Kilimanjaro (3,966 miles), Ecuador's 19,347-foot Cotopaxi (3,966.9 miles), Peru's 22,139-foot Huascaran (3,967.1 miles), and Ecuador's 20,565-foot Chimborazo (also 3,967.1 miles, but about 82 feet farther out than Huascaran). All numbers are approximate.

It wasn't until May 15, 1921, that the first official reconnaissance expedition to Everest actually started out from Darjeeling, India, 400 miles away from where they would eventually start climbing. It consisted of seventeen Sherpas, twenty-one Bhotias, two Lepchas, two Scots, five Englishmen, and one hundred government-of-India-issued mules. After five days all of the mules were either dead or abandoned to the steep and muddy Sikkimese jungle. The team bartered for what local yaks and horses they could find along the way. Every member of the expedition contracted dysentery. One died. Coincidently, he was the only one who knew how to use the crude bottled oxygen apparatus they were carrying for climbing at extreme altitude, so they abandoned it as well. It was a month before they even found Everest, spotting it for the first time on June 16 from a ridgeline 57 miles away. George Mallory, still one of Everest's most iconic legends, wrote of the experience:

We caught the gleam of snow behind the grey mists. A whole group of mountains began to appear in gigantic fragments. Mountain shapes are often fantastic seen through a mist; these were like the wildest creation of a dream. A preposterous triangular lump rose out of the depths; its edge came leaping up at an angle of about 70° and ended nowhere. To the left a black serrated crest was hanging in the sky incredibly. Gradually, very gradually, we saw the great mountainsides and glaciers and arêtes, now one fragment and now another through the floating rifts, until far higher in the sky than imagination had dared to suggest, the white summit of Everest appeared. And in this series of partial glimpses we had seen a while we were able to piece together the fragments, to interpret the dream. However much might remain to be understood, the centre had a clear meaning, as one mountain shape, the shape of Everest.

It took the expedition another three months to find a route to the base of the mountain's North Face, winding their way through the maze of boulders, melt channels, and towering 50-foot ice pinnacles called *penitentes* that make up the Rongbuk Glacier. Amazingly, they still attempted to climb the 10,000-foot wall of rock and ice they found once they got there. Even more surprising, they managed to make it up to an elevation of 23,000 feet in hobnailed leather boots, hand-cutting steps with their ice axes, wearing wool gloves, before being turned back by fierce winds, extreme cold, and frostbite. "As it is," Mallory wrote to his wife later, "we have established a way to the summit for anyone who cares to try the highest adventure."

Mallory, as it turned out, cared to try again. And again. He departed England for Tibet six months later, in early March 1922. Once in India, the team set out with over two tons of luggage. This time there were forty Sherpas, thirteen Europeans, five Gurkhas, a Tibetan interpreter, an exceedingly large and undefined number of porters, and over three hundred horses, yaks, and donkeys. The expedition ended with the climbing team reaching a new high point of 27,300 feet, just shy of the Northeast Ridge, and an avalanche sweeping seven Sherpas off a cliff to their deaths on the North Col.

The failure and gratuitous loss of life seems to have only further fanned the flames of Western enthusiasm for getting someone to the top of the mountain, however. Almost immediately, Britain requested permission from the Dalai Lama to send another expedition to the north side of Everest. It was granted, and on June 8, 1924, George Leigh Mallory found himself in Tibet for the third time, now within striking distance of the summit along with Andrew "Sandy" Irvine, a bright twenty-two-year-old engineer from Birkenhead, England, who had almost no previous climbing experience. At the time, Mallory was thirty-eight and married with three young children. A schoolmaster back home in England when he wasn't mountaineering, he and his expedition partners would read aloud from *Hamlet* and *King Lear* while tentbound. On the surface, his reasons for climbing were simple: "Because it is there," he famously retorted to a newspaper reporter who asked him why he wanted to climb Everest. Of course, his friends and colleagues had also assured him that climbing the world's tallest mountain would be good for his career as a writer and lecturer. That climbing the world's tallest mountain, and being known as the person who did it first, would give him fame and possibly even fortune.

A heavy mist blew in across the summit pyramid, prohibiting the rest of the climbing team from monitoring Mallory and Irvine's progress from below. At 12:50 p.m. the clouds parted, and their teammate Noel Odell caught a brief glimpse of the pair slowly making their way toward the top. From what he saw, they looked to be about five hours behind schedule. Then the clouds closed in, and neither Mallory nor Irvine was ever seen alive again.* No one would get as high up the mountain as they did until 1953. And it was thought for some time that no one would go higher.

In 1932 England's Captain Maurice Wilson, MC, happened on some old newspaper accounts of the 1924 Everest expedition at the same time that news of the Houston aerial expedition, which aimed to be the first to fly over Everest in an airplane, also came out. Out of this random mix of Everest-oriented suggestions, he somehow decided it would be a good idea to buy an airplane, fly it to India, crash it on the lower slopes of Everest, and then climb the tallest mountain on earth alone. With no previous flying experience he managed to navigate his Gipsy Moth *Ever Wrest* to Purnea in Bihar solo in two weeks—a stupefying, amazing act in itself. Here, despite his best efforts, he was unable to obtain official permission to fly over the forbidden kingdom of Nepal. Rather than stop his eccentric crusade, Wilson sold his airplane, proceeded to Darjeeling, recruited three Sherpas, and snuck into Tibet disguised as a Buddhist monk, similar to how Noel had snuck into the country previously. Somehow, with absolutely no mountaineering experience whatsoever, he reached the then-traditional Camp III at the North Col, one week short of a year after taking off from Edgeware, England. He died before reaching

---

* In 1999 American climber Conrad Anker found Mallory's body on a ledge at 27,000 feet. Evidence suggests that Mallory, at least, didn't make it to the summit before perishing, but no one will ever really know for sure. Andrew Irvine's body was never found.

the summit, succumbing to exhaustion and cold. The final entry in his diary read, "Off again. Gorgeous day."

In 1949, after centuries of isolation, Nepal finally opened its borders to the world. A year later, the new Communist regime in China claimed neighboring Tibet as its own and closed down all access to Everest from the north. If anyone was going to climb the mountain, it was going to have to now be from the south, accessing the base of the peak through an even more steep and harrowing-looking glacier than the Rongbuk: the Khumbu Icefall, a river of ice and stone so steep that it moves 3 to 4 feet each day, opening and closing vast crevasses, collapsing massive 50-plus-foot ice pillars every few hours.

Nepal also proved to be even less advantageous than Tibet for accessing the mountain. In the 1940s the only semblance of an entry route into the country—other than the footpaths taken by the Sherpas across mountain passes from Tibet or Sikkim—was at the Indian border railhead at Raxaul, where travelers transferred to the narrow-gauge, toylike Nepal State Railway. Using this mode of transport, it took four hours to cover around 25 miles to Amlekanj, where passengers then transferred to car or bus for a 24-mile trip that brought them up through the Shivalik mountain range and descended on the far side to the village of Bimpedi. Here, an electrically powered towrope was installed to help haul a small amount of luggage to Kathmandu over two additional mountain passes, which had to be traveled by foot. A single telephone line linked the capital to its neighbor, India.

Still, in 1953, after a few transportation improvements had been made, the third British expedition to mount an assault on Everest from the Nepal side not only managed to negotiate getting into the country, to the mountain, and up the icefall, but also made it to the top, ascending via the South Col. Just before noon on May 28, after two and a half months of climbing, setting up various camps to store supplies, a New Zealand beekeeper named Edmund Hillary and a Sherpa named Tenzing Norgay finally stood on top of Everest. It had taken over thirty years since the first attempt to climb Everest for anyone to actually make it to the summit. They stayed for fifteen minutes. Hugged one another. Took a few pictures, and left a small cross and some chocolates behind them in the snow. News reached England a few days later via a coded radio message, just in time for Queen Elizabeth's coronation. James Morris, the reporter who coded the message, later wrote in *Coronation Everest: The First Ascent and the Scoop That Crowned the Queen*:

> *It is hard to imagine now the almost mystical delight with which the coincidence of the two happenings [the coronation and the Everest ascent] was greeted in Britain. Emerging at last from the austerity which had plagued them since the second world war, but at the same time facing the loss of their great empire and the inevitable decline of their power in the world, the British had half-convinced themselves that the accession of the young Queen was a token of a fresh start —a new Elizabethan age, as the newspapers like to call it. Coronation Day, June 2, 1953, was to be a day of symbolical hope and rejoicing, in which all the British patriotic loyalties would find a supreme moment of expression: and marvel of marvels, on that very day there arrived the news from distant places—from the frontiers of the old Empire, in fact—that a British team of mountaineers . . . had reached the supreme remaining earthly objective of exploration and adventure, the top of the world . . .*
>
> *The moment aroused a whole orchestra of rich emotions among the British—pride, patriotism, nostalgia for the lost past of the war and derring do, hope for a rejuvenated future. . . . People of a certain age remember vividly to this day the moment when, as they waited on a drizzly June morning for the Coronation procession to pass by in London, they heard the magical news that the summit of the world was, so to speak, theirs.*

Hillary was knighted and became one of the most famous men on earth overnight. His image appeared on postage stamps, magazine covers, and even in comic strips. Norgay likewise became a national hero in Nepal, where the then-illiterate climber was made to sign a false statement he didn't understand claiming that he had made it to the top before Hillary.*

To this day their names, along with Mallory's and Irvine's, are inextricably linked with the idea of Everest: ordinary men—a schoolmaster, a beekeeper, an engineer with no climbing experience, and a climbing Sherpa—accomplishing, or at least attempting to achieve, the impossible. And with the idea that there is some sort of glory, or at least personal redemption, to be had in that.

Perhaps it's because people are occasionally willing to die for this idea that we listen. Everest undoubtedly still beckons.

---

* Hillary and Norgay agreed to not tell anyone who had made it to the top of Everest first. Norgay said, "It is a foolish question. The answer means nothing . . . Mountaineers understand that there is no sense to such a question; that when two men are on the same rope they are together, and that is all there is to it." Once they arrived back in Kathmandu, they both signed a public statement stating that they had "reached the summit almost together." Later, after much harassment, Norgay acknowledged that Hillary "stepped on top first. And I stepped up after him."

VI

Walking Slowly

Babu looked down at the map laid out on the short table in front of him. There was a piece of string connecting the points that represented Everest's summit and the mountain's Northwest Ridge. "Do you think we can make it?" he asked. Ryan Waters, a lanky thirty-seven-year-old American climber and professional mountain guide, sat beside him, scratching his beard. "It seems like you should be able to do it," Waters said, his breath rising in the diffused yellow light of their dome-shaped tent on the Khumbu Glacier in Everest Base Camp. Both wore puffy goose-down jackets and tight-fitting wool hats. "The math seems to work." In his hands were rough calculations for Babu and Lakpa's anticipated rate of descent from the summit once airborne, scrawled on a sheet of paper. If the math was right, Waters knew, they would be able to clear the Northwest Ridge and fly back into Nepal after launching their paraglider from the Northeast Ridge over into Tibet. If the math was wrong, they'd hit the sheer North Face of the mountain at anywhere between 20 and 50 miles per hour. "But I don't know anything about paragliding," Waters added.

"It's all good," Babu said. "It will work."

Since they had arrived at Base Camp a month earlier, Babu and Lakpa had shared Waters's camp with him and his crew. "I found out I was going to be sharing camp with them once I arrived in Kathmandu," recalls the Colorado-based climber and owner of the guide service Mountain Professionals; he was contracting the logistics of his personal expedition to Lhotse through the Kathmandu-based outfitter Himalayan Trailblazer. "I had met Lakpa in 2006 when we were both on K2. He was working as a sherpa on a Canadian expedition at the time, along with Tsering Pasong, the guy who eventually became my partner for my company's logistics. Tsering was like, 'Yeah, Lakpa is going to be with us in Base Camp.' He didn't even tell me what they were going to be doing. But that's how this group of Sherpas is. They're like a tight-knit family, so it was automatic. I was like, 'Sure, those guys can share our base camp.' I didn't even think about it."

Waters had been on three previous Everest expeditions, summiting twice, and had worked as a guide all over the Himalaya and Andes. He was recovering from a recent breakup by attempting to climb the fourth-highest mountain in the world, Lhotse, Everest's neighboring 27,940-foot peak to the east, with a thirty-two-year-old New York–based French alpinist and motivational speaker named Sophie Denis. "I was there on kind of a personal journey that spring," Waters says. "I was like, 'I just want to go to the Himalaya and go climbing, and be away from people.'" So when Lakpa showed up with Babu, who had no real climbing experience, and told him that they were going to fly off the top of Everest and then paddle to the ocean, Waters decided to just roll with it.

After celebrating the start of their journey with their friends and a few cases of Carlsburg beer at the Pokhara Pizza House, Lakpa and Babu said good-bye to their still-upset wives and children, promised to come home alive, and caught a flight to Kathmandu. They requested permits from the Nepali government to fly off Everest but were promptly denied. They were told it was illegal, despite the fact that two other foreign teams had been issued permits to fly off the summit of Everest that year already—Raineri's and Falconer's. Babu and Lakpa then hopped on a small, two-prop plane to Lukla and began the 38.5-mile walk to Everest Base Camp. They still had no paraglider, no kayak, no permits, no camera to film the movie they were supposedly making, and, in Babu's case, not even some of the basic equipment he would need to climb—namely, a climbing harness. According to Lakpa, Babu also didn't have any money.

"Babu borrowed money from friends—$100 here, $200 there—but didn't use it at all for the expedition," Lakpa says. "He gave it to his family. He came with no money from his house." Whatever happened to the $6,000 Kimberly Phinney sent Babu from the United States to help fund the expedition, Lakpa claims he doesn't know. "It's not my business," he states simply. Regardless, the two friends pressed on toward Everest.

Before leaving Kathmandu, they had managed to convince a local outdoor apparel company called Mountain Blackstone to provide them with full-body down suits, so at least they wouldn't freeze higher up on the mountain. Lakpa also contacted his friend Tsering Nima, owner of the Kathmandu-based outfitter Himalayan Trailblazer (the same one that was outfitting Waters's Lhotse expedition), at the last minute and asked him if he might be able to help, since his own cousin's outfitter, HAD, was unwilling. Nima, a longtime friend of Lakpa, told him that Himalayan Trailblazer would be happy to help by providing all of the expedition's climbing logistics, save the team's bottled oxygen, which would cost $3,000. Nima offered Lakpa the use of Waters's base camp and promised to send two climbing sherpas to help shuttle loads up the mountain. Nima then called Phu Dorji Sherpa and Nima Wang Chu, two young, low-altitude trekking guides, both of whom had climbed only once before in their lives, and asked them if they would be willing to join the expedition as climbing sherpas, without pay. Remarkably, both agreed.

"I was really excited to go," recalls Phu Dorji, a wild-haired, chain-smoking Nepali who prefers to be called by his nickname, Ang Bhai ("small boy"). He was twenty-seven years old when the opportunity arose. "I was at a movie in Kathmandu when Tsering called me and asked, 'Ang Bhai, are you interested in going to Everest?' I said, 'Of course.' After the movie I went to the Himalayan Trailblazer office, and there's Lakpa. We discussed what kind of project it is. And I'm shocked—whoa! It was really interesting. I was really happy to go."

One week later, Ang Bhai and Nima Wang Chu were on their way to Everest along with Babu and Lakpa. Ang Bhai had had his first climbing experience, working as a porter on 20,305-foot Imja Tse, only six months before. Nima Wang Chu had climbed just once before on Mera Peak, working as an assistant guide. Ang Bhai didn't have any climbing gear. "I had to get some equipment from my brother, who works as a climber," Ang Bhai says. "I didn't have good shoes. My brother gave me his shoes. They were quite big." He didn't have gloves, or a helmet either.

The path to Everest Base Camp from Lukla leads north out of town along the banks of the icy, boulder-strewn Dudh Kosi, crossing the glacial meltwater river at regular intervals over high, trembling footbridges. It then zigzags up a steep canyon wall, through a stand of tall pines that punctuates the view of Thamserku and Kusum Kangru's snowcapped peaks, 2 vertical miles above. Every inch of arable land is terraced and planted with barley, buckwheat, or potatoes. Chortens* and walls of intricately carved *mani*† stones stand quietly alongside the trail. Hundreds of porters and trekkers pass daily, carrying supplies to and from the mountains and the remote villages that lay beneath them, meandering through glades of juniper and dwarf birch, blue pine and rhododendron, past cascading waterfalls, huge boulders, and burbling streams. A few hours' walk beyond the small village of Pheriche, the path opens onto the vast glacial moraine of

* A *chorten* is a religious monument, typically made of stone and often containing sacred relics; it is also called a *stupa*.

† *Mani* stones are small, flat rocks that are hand-carved with Sanskrit symbols denoting the Tibetan Buddhist invocation *Om mani padme hum.* They are piled along the middle of trails to form long, low *mani* walls. Buddhist protocol dictates that travelers always pass *mani* walls on the left.

the Khumbu Glacier, a 12-mile-long river of ice and grinding rock tumbling down the southern flank of the mountain. At over 16,000 feet there are no trees, the trail often disappearing beneath lingering head-high winter snowpack. Chortens stand sentinel along the trail in memory of deceased climbers, mostly Sherpa. The trek ends at a small, movable city consisting of hundreds of brightly colored tents sprawled amidst the scree at the base of the Khumbu Icefall. Everest Base Camp. A quasi-permanent alpine climbing village tucked in an amphitheater of towering mountains and hanging glaciers, occupied nearly year-round by climbing teams from around the world. Each attempting to climb Everest, or one of its neighboring peaks: Lhotse, Nuptse, and Pumori. Long strings of prayer flags flap violently in the gusts of wind that rage down the mountain and through the Western Cwm.*

A strong hiker, already acclimatized to the altitude, could do the trek from the Lukla airstrip to Everest Base Camp in two or three long days. Those who are not acclimatized, like Babu and Lakpa and their two hired sherpas, generally take over a week to make the journey, in order to avoid the mind-splitting headaches and illness that accompany gaining altitude too quickly.

Lakpa knew this, having worked at altitude for so many years and with so many beginning climbers. So he decided that it would be best if, on their walk to Base Camp, he took Babu, Ang Bhai, and Nima Wang Chu off the main path and onto a side trail that leads to nearby 20,305-foot Imja Tse, also known as Island Peak—the same mountain Babu had attempted to climb with Pete Astles in 2006. His idea was for them to further acclimatize themselves to being at altitude before attempting Everest. And to see how the three other members of his expedition, who had no real practical climbing experience to speak of, fared on a relatively short and "easy" mountain. A popular "trekking

---

* Cwm (pronounced "coom") is a Welsh word for a bowl-shaped valley. It was conferred on the upper reaches of the Khumbu Glacier by the 1921 English reconnaissance expedition, the first Westerners to see it.

peak" just over 5 miles from Everest, Imja Tse has fixed lines running to the top and requires no technical climbing. "You just need crampons," Lakpa says. "No ice axe." Despite having great weather and making good time, they abandoned their summit attempt on Island Peak after Babu "got a really, really big headache at high camp," according to Ang Bhai.

Babu was concerned. It was the second time he had been at altitude, and again, he felt like a nail was being driven into his skull. It wasn't a good feeling. He asked Lakpa if he still thought he could make it to the top of Everest. "Climbing Everest is easy," Lakpa tried to reassure him. "It is just walking slowly. Up."

In a way, it was true. Ropes placed by sherpas each season lead all the way to the summit. Technically, and with a lot of luck, all anyone needs to do nowadays to get to the top is follow them. But with a searing migraine, Babu couldn't seem to even walk at altitude, let alone climb. Despite what he told Babu, Lakpa was starting to worry too. They still didn't have their paraglider, and after seeing Babu not be able to make it to the top of a relatively easy peak—9,000 feet shorter than Everest—in good weather, he knew it didn't speak well for his lowland friend's ability to function at altitude. Let alone fly a paraglider—if they ever did get one—at over 29,000 feet. "I didn't think to worry about if my pilot could walk," Lakpa says. Still, he laughed his typical deep-chested laugh and told Babu with a smile that he would get him to the top of Everest, one way or another. "You just have to get us back down," Lakpa reminded him, still laughing but serious. He meant to keep his promise to return home alive.

Back in Pokhara, Babu's boss, David Arrufat, waited patiently for his friend Richard Tan to arrive with the paragliding wing Babu and Lakpa were going to use on Everest. It had been made in a rush in France by the company Niviuk, but was being snuck into the country in Tan's luggage on an international passenger flight from Malaysia in order to avoid Nepal's nearly 200 percent import tax on the approximately $4,000 wing. It was also exceedingly late. Babu and Lakpa had been gone for over a month, already starting to climb, and the wing still wasn't even in the right country.

It had been agreed before their departure that Babu and Lakpa's twenty-nine-year-old friend Balkrishna Basel (Baloo, as his friends and family call him), a fellow Nepali tandem pilot working for another paragliding company in Pokhara, would carry the wing with him to Everest Base Camp and meet them there. The expedition's cameraman, Shri Hari Shresthra, one of Babu's childhood friends now living in Kathmandu, would meet Baloo at the capital and accompany him to Lukla and on the trail to Base Camp, carrying the camera equipment Babu and Lakpa would need to make a documentary about the expedition. This included two small, high-definition point-of-view cameras made by the company GoPro and a SPOT GPS locator, which Kimberly Phinney had mailed to Nepal from San Francisco. Lakpa agreed to pay for all of their expenses, including the new $1,000 shoulder-mount camera Shri Hari also bought to film portions of the expedition with. Baloo took up a collection amongst their friends and fellow paragliding pilots in Pokhara to help pay for the expedition's supplemental oxygen. Babu and Lakpa's trip would require, at minimum, twelve four-liter bottles (three per person) at a cost of $250 per bottle. They managed to raise nearly $1,250. It still wasn't enough to cover even half of the team's oxygen.

Come May—only three weeks before the season's projected weather window on Everest—the paraglider still hadn't arrived.

━━◆━━

Waters's camp was small compared to most. Located on the far north end of Everest Base Camp, essentially and intentionally on the outskirts, nearest to the start of the icefall, it consisted of a single large, bright yellow dome tent; a cook tent (which was really just a series of plastic tarps strung over an aluminum frame); and a few smaller, yellow dome-shaped tents for individuals to sleep in. This was because his climbing team was supposed to be small that year: just Waters, the French climber Sophie Denis, and his friend and trusted climbing sherpa from numerous past expeditions, Lakpa Dorjee. They also had two cooks: Krishna and his assistant, Mingma. They were an exceedingly small team in comparison to some of the forty-plus member expeditions nearby, including that year's International Mountain Guides (IMG) group, which consisted of almost thirty trekkers and climbers and over seventy sherpas and cooks.

When Lakpa arrived with Babu, Ang Bhai, and Nima Wang Chu, the size of Waters's camp nearly doubled. Then Waters was told Baloo and Shri Hari would be coming too, as soon as the long-awaited wing arrived in Pokhara. Waters didn't seem to mind, though. "It was good for us," he says. "At least for me—I enjoyed hanging out with them. Most nights we just ate Sherpa stew in the cook tent and drank tea." He enjoyed talking with his guests and fed off of their constant, unyielding enthusiasm. They kept all of their gear, or at least what little there was of it, in Waters's large expedition dome tent.

It took a few days, but Ang Bhai eventually managed to obtain a helmet and gloves from people leaving Base Camp who either had spares or didn't want to bother carrying the extra gear out with them. He swapped his brother's boots, which were a size too large for him and had given him painful blisters on the hike in from Lukla and on the attempt on Island Peak, for a pair that actually fit. There was still the problem of Babu not having a climbing harness, so Lakpa gave him his and donned one of the lightweight paragliding harnesses Niviuk had sent them ahead of the wing. Never intended for climbing, the harness lacked a belay loop—the fail-safe anchor point climbers attach to a rope to keep them, in the simplest terms, from falling to their death. Climbing harnesses are designed to arrest a fall generating a tremendous amount of force, like, say, plummeting off a cliff.

Inversely, the paragliding harness Lakpa had wasn't designed to stop a fall at all. If you were to fall while paragliding, there would be no rope to catch you anyway. Consequently, the harness is designed only to support the body weight of the pilot wearing it and to keep him or her attached to the wing above. This is done with two attachment points, one on either hip, rather than one in the middle of the waist, like on a climbing harness. Lacking another option, however, Lakpa took two pieces of 1-inch tubular climbing webbing, attached them to either side of his paragliding harness, and tied them together in a knot in the middle, fashioning a crude belay loop to which he could attach the Jumars (handheld mechanical devices that help climbers use ropes) he would use to ascend the fixed lines up Everest. It would work, he was certain, provided he didn't actually fall.

Every day, Lakpa called Baloo back in Pokhara on his cellular phone to check on the status of the wing, and on the boat that was supposedly being shipped from England by Babu's friend, Pete Astles, for the second half of their journey to the ocean. He used his left hand to hold the phone while his right covered his other ear to block the wind. Every day for over a month the answer was the same: Neither the wing nor the kayak was even in the country yet. They told no one at Base Camp except Waters and his team about their plans to fly off the mountain. "Their plan seemed to change day by day," Waters says. "They weren't really sure what they were going to do."

Assuming that both the wing and the kayak would eventually arrive in time to complete the expedition—the wing, meeting them at Everest Base Camp, the kayak, wherever they happened to land along the Sun Kosi River, if they managed to fly off the summit and across the Himalaya—Lakpa started his team of inexperienced climbing rookies up the mountain. He knew it would take them nearly a month to establish their higher camps—four, each approximately 2,000 feet higher than the last—and prepare their bodies for the final summit push,* which he and Babu anticipated would happen sometime at the

---

* The human body can actually "adapt" to functioning at altitude, where there are significantly less oxygen molecules in each breath, through a process called acclimatization. The act of inhaling less oxygen naturally stimulates an increase in breathing. The kidneys then begin to unload bicarbonate to compensate, and the body releases more of the hormone erythropoietin to stimulate red blood cell production, which enables the body to literally carry more oxygen. This adaptation can take many days, although up to 80% occurs in the first forty-eight to seventy-two hours.

end of May, during the annual weather window. Whenever it happened to open.

The first step would be to establish a camp above the Khumbu Icefall, the teetering, 2,000-foot wall of continually moving blocks of ice known as seracs, some the size of large buildings, and deep crevasses that inconveniently open and close without warning. The sound of its constant grinding can be heard easily from Base Camp, not far to the south. It is the most technically demanding section of the entire South Col route, which Edmund Hillary and Tenzing Norgay first used to summit the mountain in 1953: following the Khumbu Glacier up the lower part of the mountain, then cutting up the Lhotse Face to the South Col, to the Southeast Ridgeline and, eventually, the summit. From the *bergschrund** at 23,000 feet, where the glacier begins, it flows 2.5 miles down a gently sloping valley known as the Western Cwm, where it cracks and splinters in a fairly manageable and navigable way, until it tumbles spectacularly off a sheer cliff, forming the now infamous icefall. It is there that Babu, Ang Bhai, and Nima Wang Chu learned to climb. And fast.

Since the unstable seracs that make up the icefall have a tendency to shift, or just plain fall over during the heat of mid- to late afternoon, most climbers find it prudent to avoid dawdling through it. Even though the route navigating this ever-changing ice labyrinth is quite efficiently managed by an accomplished team of six sherpas known as "the Icefall Doctors," who work day and night to maintain a path through the death trap using an intricate series of fixed ropes and aluminum ladders,† there are never any guarantees of making it through safely. People die in the icefall almost every year—their bodies, if not retrieved, are crushed, dismembered, beaten, and ground by

---

* A bergschrund is a deep crevasse that delineates a glacier's upper terminus, marking the point where the ice slides away from the steeper wall immediately above, leaving a gap between the glacier and rock. Whereas a crevasse can be only a few hundred feet deep at most, there is no limit to how deep a bergschrund can go.

† Fifteen aluminum ladders were used in 2011 to negotiate the icefall, fewer than normal.

the unyielding power of the ice and deposited at the bottom, almost unrecognizable a few years later.

Babu and Lakpa were still in the middle of the icefall by late afternoon on their first day climbing in mid-April. Babu could hardly breathe, had a searing headache, and had to stop to rest every few feet. Lakpa wasn't sure what to do. They would need to travel through the icefall at least eight to ten more times before summiting. And they would need to do it much, much faster if they weren't going to die, let alone stand a chance of getting to the top. He also knew it was only going to get harder for Babu to function the higher they went, and that they intended to go even higher than the summit with the paraglider. He needed Babu to get over his altitude sickness. Quick.

Babu, likewise, was becoming disheartened. He asked Waters, who had by now become a good friend, after days of drinking tea and discussing climbing together, if he thought he could make it. "No problem, Babu," Waters always told him. "You can make it." He liked Babu. "He's one of the nicest, most genuine people I've ever met," Waters says. He wanted him to succeed.

Ang Bhai and Nima Wang Chu were left to themselves to shuttle loads up to Camp I, and each succeeding camp. They left the first day at 3:00 a.m., following another group of hired climbing sherpas who were also shuttling loads up the icefall. "The first time I went through the Khumbu Icefall, I was really scared," Ang Bhai says, recalling the experience. "Really scared. I didn't know what's going on. I didn't know anything. The whole time, I walked behind other people, because I didn't know the way. I didn't want to get lost, so I followed them."

After carrying his first load—a single tent—up the icefall in strong winds, Ang Bhai was completely wrecked. "I spent two days after that in Base Camp with a really big headache," he says. Of the four members of the climbing team, two were suffering severely from altitude sickness. Only Lakpa and Nima Wang Chu seemed to be able to even mildly function, even at the base of Everest.

After they carried enough gear to the top of the icefall to set up at Camp I, they spent four days shuttling even more gear 1.74 miles and approximately 1,500 vertical feet up the glacier through an area known as the Western Cwm to Camp II, directly below the Lhotse Face. During the day temperatures in the cwm soared above 100 degrees Fahrenheit, the sunlight reflecting off the snow-white faces of Lhotse, Nuptse, and Everest and off the Khumbu Glacier itself. Being caught in the middle in the sun was like being an ant caught beneath a mountain valley–size magnifying glass. Babu and Ang Bhai felt terrible. They were losing weight and having a difficult time sleeping. The weather was also becoming an issue. The jet stream wasn't moving an inch. The summit was still being blasted by 100-mile-per-hour winds, even with the onset of the monsoon in the Indian subcontinent and Indian Ocean, which in the past had always pushed the river of fast-moving air that was still raging at the summit just slightly to the north. There was some speculation in Base Camp of a split in the jet stream, part north and part south, but no one actually knew what was going on, or what was going to happen. According to Alan Arnette— a fifty-four-year-old member of the IMG expedition that year, an experienced mountaineer, and "one of the most respected voices on Everest," according to *Outside* magazine—"The weather was proving almost impossible to predict using the usual models. Forecasters threw out some models and refined others as the season progressed, but by [then] teams had become skeptical of their usually reliable weather partners."

Eventually, a tentative break in the weather was announced for May 15. Rodrigo Raineri, the Brazilian who was attempting to paraglide off the top of the mountain, and Squash Falconer, the British woman who was about to attempt the same feat, both mobilized their teams for a summit bid. Babu and Lakpa still didn't even have their paraglider. And Babu could hardly walk.

Still, Babu and Lakpa decided to push on to Camp III and spend a night, in order to be fully acclimatized for their eventual summit push.

Camp III is perched high on the steep South Face of Lhotse, at about 24,000 feet. To get there one must climb a steep, 20- to 50-degree wall of hard-packed snow and ice with the assistance of several 200-foot-long fixed lines placed, of course, by sherpas. Even with the fixed lines, it's a difficult, risky proposition. On May 1 a fifty-five-year-old climber on the IMG team named Rick Hitch simply collapsed while ascending to Camp III. He never regained consciousness. The exact cause of his death is still unknown.

Babu was still uncertain whether he could make it. His altitude sickness, which Lakpa had kept telling him would eventually go away, wasn't going away. Back at Base Camp, he asked Waters again, "Do you think I can make it to Camp III?" Waters, not entirely certain himself but not wanting to upset his friend, told him he thought he could. Babu made it to Camp III, but on the way back to Base Camp he began to hallucinate in the middle of the icefall. He later said he saw "five ropes instead of one." Other climbers started laughing at him, he says. They allegedly thought he was dancing. *Shit, I'm not dancing,* Babu thought to himself. *I can't see straight!*

He was trying to avoid some invisible threat when he was already standing on a very real one.

On May 8 the specialty ultralight wing from France finally arrived in Pokhara, free of taxes. That same morning, Squash Falconer departed Base Camp for her final summit push and her own attempt at launching a paraglider off the top of Everest. Like most everyone else on the mountain, she wasn't aware that Babu and Lakpa were actually intending to fly off of it before her.

⊷ ⊶

Back at the Blue Sky Paragliding office, Arrufat used a stencil to spray-paint the logo of his professional paragliding organization, the APPI, onto the white and red fabric of the wing, filling in the parts he missed with a black permanent marker. Baloo then caught a flight to Kathmandu with the wing, where he met Shri Hari, a bespectacled, smart-looking Nepali with wavy, slicked-back black hair. Shri Hari had grown up in a small mountain village just three hours from Babu and had flown across Nepal from east to west in a tandem paraglider with him in 2010, in twenty-one days, unsupported. He had filmed the journey and intended to make a full documentary about the adventure, which he had yet to complete. At Babu's prompting, Lakpa hired him as the cameraman for their impromptu Everest expedition. Once in Kathmandu, Baloo and Shri Hari boarded the next available flight to Lukla. It took them four days to reach Everest Base Camp.

Baloo, a handsome young man with gentle eyes and a soft voice, put the wing in a regular trekking backpack along with some of his clothes to disguise it from the police. "There are very strict police checks in some places," he says. "If they had known, there would have been some trouble." Babu and Lakpa didn't have permits for what they were doing.

After arriving at Base Camp, Baloo and Shri Hari both became ill with altitude sickness. They had gained too much altitude too quickly, rushing their approach from Lukla in order to deliver the wing to Babu and Lakpa before Raineri or Falconer could launch off the mountain. According to Baloo, he and Shri Hari had also spent a good deal of time drinking "Sherpa Roxy," a whiskeylike grain alcohol, during their rush to reach Base Camp. "We were already dehydrated from the altitude," he recalls. "I think the whiskey only made us more dry." Baloo developed a wicked headache and a persistent cough. Happy that their wing had actually arrived, even though the other two paragliders were already on their way to the summit, the team spent their last few "rest" nights in camp dancing, drinking, and playing loud Nepali music out of the small Chinese CD player Lakpa had brought from his home in Kathmandu.

According to Ang Bhai, whose patience was beginning to run thin with Babu and Lakpa's lack of planning and what he viewed as their complete lack of regard for his safety, "They were always laughing and singing. They were not serious. I work with French people. I know how if a foreigner is doing a project like this, they are really serious. But Lakpa and Babu are not serious. All the time, they're laughing." Ang Bhai asked them, frustrated, scared, and a bit desperate, "Be serious, please. This is not game." Babu and Lakpa told him to relax. That everything would be fine.

━ ━

The urge to be the "first" to do something on Everest is by no means new, although it is becoming increasingly difficult to achieve. Since Hillary and Norgay summited via the South Col in 1953, nearly eighteen new routes have been established to the top. Somewhere around 3,668 people have reached the summit, many more than once. Reinhold Messner and Peter Habeler became the first to climb to the top without supplemental oxygen in 1978, a feat long thought simply impossible. Since then, dozens of people have done it. As Maurice Isserman and Stewart Weaver point out in *Fallen Giants*, a definitive history of mountaineering in the Himalaya:

> *Himalayan mountaineers required new measures of achievement . . . the most common form of record making was that based on identity: becoming the first female or first climber of this or that nationality to reach the summit of this or that peak. Everest, as always, was the most desired destination. Thus Bachendri Pal became the first Indian woman to climb Everest in 1984, Stacy Allison the first American woman to do so in 1988, and Rebecca Stephens the first British woman to do so in 1993. In 1989 Ricardo Torres became the first Mexican (and the first Latin American) to reach Everest's summit, and in 1995 Nasuh Mahruki the first Turk (and the first Muslim) to do so. There were also family firsts: in 1990 Marija and Andrej Stremfelj were the first married couple to reach Everest's summit together, followed two years later by the first pair of brothers to climb the mountain together, Alberto and Felix Inurrategui.*

After someone from every possible variation of national and personal identity had managed to reach the summit, age suddenly became a notable factor, creating a race for both the youngest and oldest person to reach the summit.* The youngest currently to have done it was thirteen years old when he made it to the top. The oldest: eighty.

An eighty-two-year-old Nepali named Shailendra Kumar Upadhyay was actually attempting to break the record again in 2011. He died on May 9, shortly after sharing tea with Babu and Lakpa, collapsing suddenly in the snow on his way from Camp I back to Base Camp.

As more firsts were accomplished, more people kept dying. From 1924 to 2013, a total of 249 people lost their lives on Everest (162 Westerners and 87 sherpas). Within that time span activities outside of traditional mountaineering—that is to say, trying to just get to the top of a peak and then back down again, safely—started showing up on Everest. In 1970 Japan's Yuichiro Miura attempted to ski down the Lhotse Face from below the South Col, using a small parachute to help control his descent. He crashed spectacularly and tumbled completely out of control the final 600 feet before coming to rest on the glacier below. Miura survived. Six of his expedition's sherpas, who were swept away in an avalanche, did not. The documentary film made about the expedition, *The Man Who Skied Down Everest,* won an Academy Award and was eventually turned into a book. Since then, multiple people have skied, snowboarded, paraglided, and even BASE jumped off the slopes and from the summit of the mountain; of course those feats include Jean-Marc Boivin's solo paragliding descent from the top in 1988 and Claire and Zebulon Roche's tandem descent in 2001. In 2007 the Nepal Mountaineering Association actually found it prudent to call for a ban on "nudity and attempts to set obscene records" on the mountain after a Nepali climber stood stark naked on the summit for

---

* In 2010 a thirteen-year-old boy from Big Bear, California, named Jordan Romero became the youngest person to make the summit, ousting the previous record holder, Nepal's Temba Sheri, who climbed to the top at the age of sixteen. In 2013 eighty-year-old Yuichiro Miura claimed the title for the oldest person to have summited, ousting the previous record holder, who was seventy-six. Miura had summited twice before, each time earning himself the title of oldest person to summit Everest.

several minutes the year before and a Dutch man attempted to climb the peak wearing shorts.

Babu and Lakpa weren't aware of most of these firsts, however. They were still convinced that they were going to be the first to paraglide from the summit, and that they were going to claim that first for Nepal—if they could only beat Falconer and Raineri to it.

— ◦ —

Squash Falconer found herself standing on the summit of Everest at 8:30 a.m. on May 12, completely surrounded by white. The air temperature was -50 degrees Fahrenheit, the wind gusting up to 35 miles per hour. She had been climbing for over eleven hours. The Brazilian paraglider Rodrigo Raineri had already decided to call off his summit attempt and descend from Camp IV, after suffering frostbite on his toes.

"I knew that there would be no flight from the top of the world," Falconer would write later on her blog. "I was feeling wrecked. I took out my GoPro camera and filmed for a few seconds, my hand got so cold that was all I could manage. Then I was just desperate to get back down. I'd had so many plans for the summit; so many poses to do for the camera, so much I was going to say, flags I was going to get out, small dances I was going to do to celebrate . . . I'd even half planned how I would feel—so elated, amazing, wonderful . . . . but there was none of that. I was worried that I wasn't going to make it back down and after just a few short minutes at the top I was out of there." She spent the next five hours descending in blizzard conditions to Camp IV, where she crawled into her tent and passed out for twelve hours. At the same time, an experienced fifty-nine-year-old climber from Japan named Takashi Ozaki died 835 feet from the summit after suffering from a severe case of altitude sickness.

The next day, Falconer unpacked the paraglider her sherpas had carried for her and attempted to take off from the South Col in strong winds. "I thought I could give it a go," she later wrote. "I soon decided after being dragged about the mountain that it was definitely better to just get back down alive."

With Raineri and Falconer out of the running, Babu, Lakpa, Ang Bhai, and Nima Wang Chu prepared for their own summit attempt. Recognizing the fact that he had never actually flown at anywhere even near the altitude of Everest's summit, though, Babu figured it might be a good idea to take the new wing for a test flight first. They took the backpack they had stashed in the corner of Waters's dome tent, which had been hiding the paraglider along with some of Baloo's dirty clothes, and walked two hours south out of Base Camp. Here, they climbed a small, 33-foot promontory called Kala Patthar (meaning "black rock") to the south of Pumori, a sharp, dangerous-looking mountain. A long, lingering plume of snow could be seen blowing off the summit of Everest in the distance. The sun was high and hot in the sky. Babu unfolded the new wing and instructed Nima Wang Chu on how to help him launch it, which he had never done before, by first holding it tight to the ground and then lifting it so the wind could catch it once Babu was ready to take off. This, he was told, would be his job on summit day. Ang Bhai would be responsible for holding the camera, which Shri Hari was holding now.

The wing inflated easily in the gentle breeze blowing through the valley that morning, making a large red crescent shape against the stark white, black, and blue jagged landscape. Babu flew solo in a single wide, sweeping arc, landing back at the top of the promontory where he had taken off. The flight lasted about thirty seconds. After landing he immediately repacked the wing in Baloo's backpack. They didn't want to draw too much attention to themselves. The brief inaugural flight of the new wing felt different than flying in Pokhara, or anywhere else Babu had ever flown in Nepal. "It was fast," Babu recalls, noting the increased rate of descent resultant from the wing struggling to catch loft in the thin air found at over 18,500 feet. "Really fast."

Suddenly and unexpectedly, at 9:00 a.m. on May 15, another brief weather window was projected for the morning of May 21. Base Camp was buzzing with renewed excitement. Unfortunately, the winds were expected to increase again significantly in the afternoon that same day. Not a good thing when attempting to launch a paraglider from the top of Everest. Still, Lakpa and Babu decided this would be the window they would shoot for. They just needed to get to the top and then fly back down to the bottom before the wind started up, they determined. "No problem," Lakpa said.

The gear for their final summit push was sprawled out on the floor of Waters's dome tent. Seeing that Babu and Lakpa had packed only rice and beans for themselves, Waters gave them a few of his freeze-dried meals along with a handful of Snickers candy bars before they set out from Base Camp. He also gave Lakpa one of his extra pairs of goggles, noticing the experienced guide didn't have any. After climbing for what would hopefully be their final time through the icefall, with Ang Bhai carrying the few bottles of oxygen that were left to be shuttled up the mountain and Nima Wang Chu carrying the new wing, they spent a night at Camp II. Lakpa and Babu were together in one tent, Nima Wang Chu and Ang Bhai in another. At Camp III the next night, both Ang Bhai and Nima Wang Chu had to stay in the tents of sherpas working for other teams, as their own team had only one tent set up at both Camp III and Camp IV.

For an entire day gale-force winds blasted the Lhotse Face, causing the four of them to lean against the tent poles in order to support them so they wouldn't snap. Snow piled up, drifting on the tents, causing the walls to sag precariously inward. With the wind, it was determined to be too dangerous to go outside and attempt to shovel it off. A constant howling and flapping of fabric berated them. They didn't sleep at all and began using their bottled oxygen to help alleviate their altitude sickness, which both Babu and Ang Bhai were still feeling significantly. Lakpa, meanwhile, was still smoking cigarettes.

The climb from Camp III to Camp IV on the South Col is only 0.8 miles, but it takes anywhere from three to six hours and reaches an elevation of 26,300 feet, an elevation affectionately known amongst climbers as the Death Zone, where human beings can't survive more than two or three days, no matter how well they've managed to acclimatize beforehand. After an hour or so of steep but easy climbing up the rest of the Lhotse Face, there is a band of rock accurately, if not creatively, coined the Yellow Band: a large yellow-colored strip of limestone running through the Himalaya, created millions of years earlier at the bottom of an ancient ocean. Here, the route to the South Col leaves the snow and ice of the Lhotse Face and climbs around 300 feet of smooth rock sitting at a 20- to 30-degree angle. Here, too, there are fixed lines conveniently set up by sherpas, to keep people from tripping and falling to their death. Once clear of the band, the mountain actually flattens out somewhat until the bottom of the ridge defining the South Col, which is placed rather breathtakingly between the summits of Everest and Lhotse. Before reaching the col, however, climbers must first navigate an area known as the Geneva Spur: 150 feet of slanting, 40-degree rock, ice, and snow. Topping the ridge, a narrow, rocky path leads to the South Col proper, an area the size of approximately two football fields. At the far west end, thirty bright yellow and orange tents sit huddled together, clinging to the mountain.

Ang Bhai and Nima Wang Chu ran multiple loads up to Camp IV without Lakpa or Babu, preparing camp for them, escorted by other sherpas working on that part of the mountain that day. Miraculously, both Babu and Ang Bhai started to get somewhat over their altitude sickness. On May 20 Ang Bhai, who had spent the night at Camp II after running loads to the higher camps for Lakpa and Babu, climbed all the way to Camp IV in order to meet the rest of the team in time for their summit push, which was scheduled to begin that night. "There was a lot of people," he says. "I just followed them."

Once all of them were in Camp IV, they huddled together in one tent, not sleeping but trying to rest, drinking as much water and eating as much food as they could as they waited for dark. They knew it would take them all night, and well into the next morning, to make the summit. They wanted to leave in the middle of the night, like most teams do, so they could arrive early enough to miss the strong winds and storms that generally rear up on top of Everest later in the day, especially since they were anticipated to be particularly bad the next day.

"There was too much wind," Ang Bhai says. "We only had one tent. Four people." They were low on food and had forgotten about the Snickers bars, which were now frozen solid at the bottom of one of their bags. They made black tea with no sugar. As the wind howled around them, crows circled overhead, looking for scraps to eat in the otherwise desolate and sterile white wasteland of the South Col. By the time the wind died at around 10:30 p.m., they were more than ready to leave. Before departing, however, Lakpa made an extra-strong batch of coffee, as he typically did before every summit push. It was the first time Babu had ever tried coffee. "It was great," Babu remembers. His altitude sickness seemed to almost immediately disappear. "I couldn't keep up with him," Ang Bhai says. Babu practically ran up the rest of the mountain.

The summit itself is about 1.07 miles from the South Col and Camp IV. It usually takes climbers about eight to ten hours to make the journey, which first ascends a steep triangular face to a small platform at 27,600 feet known simply as the Balcony. Continuing up the ridge is a series of slippery rock slabs. In "good" snow years—that is to say, in years when there is enough snow to cover the slabs, but not so much as to be overly cumbersome—this section is fairly straightforward and safe, particularly with the use of the fixed lines. However, 2011 was not a good snow year. "It was dangerous," Lakpa says. After the rock slabs the route gets even steeper for about 100 feet, nearing an angle of almost 60 degrees, depositing finally on the South Summit.

From here, climbers descend about 50 feet to a particularly dicey-looking knife-edge ridge. On one side is an 11,000-foot sheer drop down the Kangshung Face. On the other, an 8,000-foot void falling down the mountain's Southwest Face. The path itself is compacted snow loosely adhered to, likewise, loose rock. After the Cornice Traverse, as this ridge is called, there is a noticeable and unavoidable wall of rock, ice, and snow. This, Hillary described in 1953, when he and Norgay became the first to summit, as "the most formidable-looking problem on the ridge—a rock step some 40 feet high.... The rock itself, smooth and almost holdless, might have been an interesting Sunday afternoon problem to a group of expert climbers in the Lake District, but here it was a barrier beyond our feeble strength to overcome." Still roped to Norgay, Hillary wedged himself between a crack in the rock and a vertical wall of snow and began slowly, strenuously, wiggling his way up. The climbing was sketchy at best. He and Norgay made it to the top, though, of course, and from then on the wall has been known as the Hillary Step.

Nowadays, ropes set annually by sherpas run from the top to bottom, and climbers use mechanical ascenders to aid themselves in overcoming the obstacle. At the top of the Hillary Step, sitting on a ledge, rests a large chockstone blocking the path to the summit. It's easy to scoot around, but there's a 1,000-foot drop if you fall. A series of small, permanently snow-covered bumps leads to and blocks the view of the summit. To the right, snow cornices formed by the prevailing winds cling tenuously to the mountainside, waiting for someone to step on them and set them tumbling. The summit itself is no more than 30 square feet, marked with strings of continually flapping bright red, blue, and yellow prayer flags and, in 2011, a dug-out snow bench on which the victorious could sit and pose for pictures. Then, aside from the magnificent view, there's nothing—just sky and the vast expanse of the Himalaya stretching off into the distance, disappearing over a curved horizon.

After nearly ten hours of climbing, Lakpa, Babu, Nima Wang Chu (who was carrying the wing), and Ang Bhai reached the summit at approximately 8:15 a.m. on May 21. Ang Bhai, who didn't have any expedition mitts for his hands, wore thin fleece gloves, soaked through and now frozen. His hands were spared severe frostbite only by a pair of hand warmers given to him before the expedition by his brother, who had also given him boots and had lost several of his own digits after working for years as a climbing sherpa in the Himalaya.

On their way up, Babu and Lakpa had stopped to talk with another Nepali climber who was on his way down from the summit, a man named Bhakta Kumar Rai. The thirty-year-old had just spent thirty-two hours on the top of the world in a small tent, meditating—the longest anyone has spent on the top and still lived to tell about it. He introduced himself as "Supreme Master God Angel" and allegedly told Babu that he would one day be president of Nepal.

After taking a few pictures of themselves standing at the summit holding pictures of their families, the Nepali flag, and a banner for Arrufat's APPI, Babu, Lakpa, Ang Bhai, and Nima Wang Chu walked down the opposing Northeast Summit Ridge. They stopped on a small, gently sloping snow platform placed precariously between a 10,000-foot drop into Tibet and an 11,000-foot drop down the Kangshung Face—the same place, coincidentally, the Roches had launched their tandem paraglider in 2001. Here, the Nepalis unpacked their wing, which took nearly an hour, and waited for the wind to die down before they attempted to take flight.

———

Clouds rolled slowly through the lesser mountains to the north. Babu looked up at a brilliant cold blue sky, feeling suddenly light-headed. It wasn't just vertigo; he realized he had run out of supplemental oxygen. His body was beginning to shut down. Lakpa, standing in front of him and attached at the waist by a pair of locking carabiners, took his last remaining bottle, which he was using, and hooked it up to Babu's regulator. Lakpa turned it on full flow, deciding that he wanted the man who would be piloting the paraglider to stay awake during its upcoming flight.

They were no longer laughing or joking. No one was joking. There was just the sound of the wind howling in their ears, with the sky above and the world below.

Babu, feeling only slightly more coherent, began to pray.

During a brief lull in the wind, Babu told Nima Wang Chu, who had been holding the wing firmly to the snow behind them, unroped on an overhanging cornice, to lift it up and launch it. Babu and Lakpa took a step forward in unison, toward the 10,000-foot drop into Tibet in front of them. The wing suddenly caught an updraft, taking off like a kite. Their feet lifted off the ground. For a moment the two were airborne. Then they crashed, landing exactly, and extraordinarily, right where they had been standing a moment earlier.

Getting up from the snow, apparently unfazed, Babu yelled over to Ang Bhai, who was still roped in to the fixed line leading up the Northeast Ridge to the summit, crouched behind a boulder, holding a small video camera. Babu told him to unrope and help Nima Wang Chu launch the wing. If he helped Nima, Babu knew, there would be no footage of him and Lakpa taking off from the top of Everest, except for what was being recorded on the small GoPro camera dangling from Babu's left wrist, attached to a stick. He didn't care.

"Run," he told Lakpa. Firmly. Without yelling. "Run."

PART II

THE DESCENT

VII

In Flight

Fifty Feet over Everest,
May 21, 2011—29,085 Feet

A small crowd had gathered around an old desktop computer in the home of David Arrufat and his girlfriend, Wildes, outside of Pokhara. Babu's wife, Susmita, and their two young sons, seven-year-old Niraj and four-month-old Himalaya, as well as Lakpa's wife, Yanjee, and their four-year-old son, Mingma Tashi, anxiously peered over one another's shoulders to get a better view, although they weren't quite sure what they were looking at. The tiny yellow dot flickering on the screen, which supposedly represented Babu and Lakpa's exact GPS location, transmitted by the SPOT locator device they were carrying, hadn't moved in nearly thirty-seven minutes. It was fixed on a sloping ledge, partway up the North Face of Everest. Not moving.

"Everything looked like it had gone wrong," Wildes, a dark-haired, brown-eyed, slow-speaking Brazilian says. Her boyfriend and Babu's paragliding mentor, David, put his head in his hands. It was going to be difficult explaining to the children that their fathers were now dead.

Then, suddenly, the dot moved, jumping several miles to the south, to a spot just north of the small mountain village of Namche Bazaar, where Babu and Lakpa actually were floating blithely down toward the nearby Syangboche airstrip, singing loudly, exceedingly pleased they hadn't died, and completely unaware that their GPS tracker had stopped working almost immediately after takeoff when they had entered Chinese airspace.*

The takeoff from the summit ridge had gone surprisingly well, all things considered. Lakpa couldn't breathe for the first thirty seconds of the flight. "It felt like someone was choking me," he says. After inflating the wing, an updraft ripping up the North Face had launched him and Babu 50 feet straight into the air—their crampons dangling beneath them along with 10,050 feet of exposure, the Rongbuk Glacier stretching off into the distance nearly 2 miles below.

Lakpa, who had chosen to skip breakfast that morning in favor of a cigarette, and who had given his last bottle of oxygen to Babu, simply couldn't get enough air in his lungs anymore. He had used supplemental oxygen on all three of his previous successful summit bids. Now he was suspended even higher than the summit of Everest with none. He was so out of it he didn't bother attaching his small GoPro camera to his helmet like he had planned. He didn't even turn it on, figuring the 5.9-ounce camera would be too heavy on his head, which he was already struggling to hold up.

Babu, who was piloting the wing with Lakpa sitting in his lap, held their other GoPro in his left hand, attached to a telescoping plastic rod. However, since he needed both hands to hold on to the brake lines above his head in order to control the paraglider, the rod dangled from his wrist with the camera rolling.

As they continued to rise, Lakpa felt an invisible hand tightening around his neck. With what air he had left in his lungs he shouted at Babu, who was distracted by a desperate attempt to control their rapid

---

* According to the SPOT website, Everest itself lies within an area of "reduced or no coverage available within a 20 minute period." It's impossible to say for certain what, exactly, caused Babu and Lakpa's device to malfunction almost immediately after takeoff, since numerous factors can scramble a GPS signal. However, considering that the handheld unit they were using was trying to communicate with four separate satellites orbiting the earth at a height of about 11,500 miles, traveling at approximately 9,000 miles per hour in different directions, while Babu and Lakpa were simultaneously flying over Everest, it would have been more surprising if it had worked.

ascent, "Oxygen! Oxygen! Oxygen!" The last bottle Babu was using, which was keeping him from choking and passing out in the thin air, was almost empty. They needed to descend, he knew. Immediately.

⌒

Lakpa and Babu's current predicament was not an entirely new one. In 1862 two English scientists named Henry Coxwell and James Glaisher actually became the first people to fly above 29,000 feet without the aid of supplemental oxygen. It was not on purpose. And it did not go well. The pair took off at 1:00 p.m. on September 5 from Wolvering-hampton, England, in a wicker basket attached to a 90,000-cubic-foot hydrogen-filled balloon. Overhead, a solid cloud deck loomed (in hindsight, ominously). They were dressed in simple wool suits, befitting their scholarly professions and the chilly autumn day. Their plan: rise to an elevation of approximately 26,000 feet, recording temperature and humidity levels along the way, then climb up into the overhead rigging and pull the gas release line and descend. In spite of the fact that no one at the time actually knew how the human body would react to being at extreme altitude, Coxwell and Glaisher smartly anticipated the air expanding and thus thinning as they climbed, and guessed, quite rightly, that it might present them a problem once they were about 5 miles up. So they decided that's when they would call it quits and descend.

Things started off well enough. The pair climbed steadily toward the clouds, beginning to handwrite their measurements at precisely 1:03 p.m. Coxwell would later write about the experience, saying, "On emerging from the cloud at seventeen minutes past one, we came into a flood of light, with a beautiful blue sky without a cloud above us, and a magnificent sea of cloud below, its surface being varied with endless hills, hillocks, mountain chains and many snow white masses rising from it." He tried to take a picture, but the silver bromide crystals in the film he was using didn't expose right. After nineteen minutes they reached an altitude of about 10,560 feet. The temperature, as they had predicted, was dropping—a lot faster than expected. The two mildly overweight forty-three-year-olds also noted having a newfound shortness of breath. Hypoxia, which is what they were suffering from, wasn't a concept fully understood in the Victorian era. At just over 21,000 feet, they began having trouble writing down their measurements. Their hands, they also noted, were freezing.

After forty-seven minutes Coxwell and Glaisher reached their planned maximum altitude, just under 29,000 feet. The temperature was -30 degrees Fahrenheit. Frostbite was setting in on every part of their bodies that was exposed to the air. They were gasping for breath and feeling precariously light-headed. They realized, suddenly, that they could no longer even read their instruments. Glaisher noted that he didn't seem to have any control over his arms and legs, shortly before passing out.

It was at this moment, after seeing his cohort slip unexpectedly into unconsciousness, that Coxwell decided it would be prudent of him to begin their descent. Without the use of his now-frozen hands, Coxwell somehow clambered his way up the rope rigging supporting their wicker basket, grabbed the gas release line between his teeth, and pulled three times. Just enough hydrogen was released from the balloon to initiate their descent and thus save both of their lives. It took Glaisher seven minutes to regain consciousness, at which point he resumed taking notes.

No one went higher for some time. And when they did, they brought their own bottled oxygen.

The first flyover of Everest occurred on April 3, 1933, twenty years before Tenzing Norgay and Edmund Hillary would actually stand on the peak's summit. Two biplanes (Westland PV3s, to be exact) piloted by Lieutenant David McIntyre and Sir Douglas Douglas-Hamilton (the Marquis of Clydesdale) took off from Purnea in Bihar, India, about 160 miles to the southeast of Everest, attempting to survey the entire region through a series of "survey strip" photographs. The flights went routinely, aside from one photographer's oxygen supply temporarily failing and Lord Clydesdale flying daringly, and entirely unnecessarily, through the ice plume blowing off of Everest's summit. They cleared the peak by 100 feet. The surveying part of the mission unfortunately and predictably failed, however, the lower part of the Himalaya being covered in its usual dusty haze, which rises up from the southern plains, obscuring most all of the lesser peaks on a daily basis. The flight didn't set an altitude record, since planes at that time had already flown up to 40,000 feet. Just not over Everest.

No one bothered to fly over the mountain again until 1988, when Jean-Marc Boivin launched his paraglider off the summit. And he, technically, just flew down from the top, not over it—a fairly random, arbitrary distinction, but a distinction nonetheless. The same is true for Claire and Zebulon Roche, when they launched their tandem wing from the summit in 2001 and glided straight down to the Rongbuk Glacier below.

In 2004 a well-known Italian aviator named Angelo D'Arrigo ("the Human Condor") attempted to fly over the summit in a hang glider, after being towed into position by a small microlight plane. After reaching an altitude of well over 26,000 feet, the towrope snapped. Angelo reported afterward: "We were at a height of about 9,000 meters, I was 500m south of Everest. I released what was left of the towrope and headed for the peak, flying over it soon after." In the video footage of the flight, captured by a camera mounted on the wing, you can see D'Arrigo being shaken like a rag doll, the high winds and turbulence near the summit making him lose complete control over the glider more than once. D'Arrigo, who had trained in a wind tunnel for the stunt and used supplemental oxygen for his flight, also lacked a GPS track log. To this day, no one knows for sure exactly how high he went.

In 2007 the British adventurer, author, and popular television personality Edward "Bear" Grylls went so far as to attempt flying over Everest using a paramotor.* After hauling all of his equipment along

* *Paramotor* is a generic name for a motorized paraglider, typically propelled by a large fan mounted to the frame in which the pilot sits.

with a film crew to within 8 miles of the mountain, however, he didn't actually fly over the peak; the Chinese government resolutely refused to issue him a permit to enter their airspace. Still, he managed to reach an altitude of approximately 29,500 feet with the aid of bottled oxygen and endured temperatures up to -76 degrees Fahrenheit, flying his paramotor just to the south of the mountain over Nepal.

The only other person to have flown directly over the summit was Didier Delsalle, who in 2005 allegedly went so far as to actually land an Ecureuil/AStar AS 350 B3 helicopter on the top. Likewise, he was breathing supplemental oxygen.

Aside from Coxwell and Glaisher, Lakpa was more than likely only the third person to ever experience dangling over 29,000 feet in the air with no motor and no bottled oxygen. And he didn't have a gas release cord to pull.

———

Babu pulled hard on the brake lines above his head, hoping to direct the wing out of the edge of the updraft that was threatening to blast him and Lakpa into the stratosphere. Lakpa, now completely out of air, could no longer scream. Then, almost as quickly as they had taken off, they began to drop, the enormous wing above them struggling to catch enough purchase to support both of their weight in the thin air.

With precision Babu directed them back toward the summit, passing directly over it. Their GPS tracker later reported that they had reached a maximum altitude of 29,085 feet, making it the unofficial highest free flight ever.*

---

* Babu and Lakpa never actually applied for a world record attempt through the Fédération Aéronautique Internationale (FAI), the Swiss governing body that manages all paragliding and hang gliding record keeping. Therefore they didn't receive an official "world record" for their flight over Everest, which, indeed, went a bit higher than both Jean-Marc Boivin's and Claire and Zebulon Roche's. Interestingly, the FAI doesn't even recognize any free flight world altitude record. According to FAI Record Officer Christine Rousson, "Only records listed in the Sporting Code, Section 7 are permitted." And the record for who goes the highest while strapped to a paraglider isn't in that section. It isn't in any section. So Boivin and the Roches never, technically, held that record either. No one has.

After dropping back down below the level of the summit, Lakpa regained his ability to breathe. He began to sing. Loudly. What song, he doesn't remember. "I sing when I'm happy," he says. And he was happy he wasn't dead. Babu said nothing, completely focused on flying the wing in conditions he had never experienced before. Still, he did it with one hand, holding the telescoping rod mounted with the still-running GoPro camera out in front of him. He switched it from hand to hand occasionally, to capture them flying from different angles. Lakpa pulled a small digital still camera out of his pocket and began taking pictures. He also started filming with the small handheld video recorder.

They flew across the West Ridge, clearing it by several hundred feet, as Waters and Babu had predicted they would. Lakpa, looking back on Everest from above, had a sudden moment of *déjà vu*. Although he knew he had never seen Everest from this angle, which had always either been above him or directly under his boots, he shouted back at Babu, "I have seen this once before!" *Yes*, Lakpa was certain, *I have seen this before in my dreams.* And this thought made him even happier. He continued singing as they reached the Khumbu Icefall.

Here, Babu turned them southwest, crossing the massive flank of 25,791-foot Nuptse, still well above 23,000 feet. Lakpa, still singing; Babu, silent and filming. They continued in a straight line, crossing above the summit of 19,049-foot Pokalde Peak and past the snowy ramparts of 22,349-foot Ama Dablam to the narrow gravel runway known as the Syangboche airstrip. Their crampons scraped loudly against the small rocks of the gravel runway as they landed, still wearing their full-body down suits. They unceremoniously folded up the wing, put it back in an unmarked, black non-paraglider-looking backpack, unzipped their down suits so they wouldn't overheat, and walked into town.

⌐•—•⌐

No one was there to greet them when they landed. Shri Hari Shresthra, their cameraman, was still at Base Camp, a full day's walk away, waiting for them to arrive there. Babu and Lakpa had not bothered to discuss with Shri Hari where, exactly, they were going to land. He had assumed they were just going to fly back down to Base Camp; he wasn't expecting them to land over 12 miles away from his lens. But in hindsight, Lakpa says, "We didn't know where we were going to land."

Few climbers on the mountain even noticed what had just happened over their heads. Those who did notice, like Damian Benegas, the Argentinian expedition leader who was standing on the summit along with two of his clients, could do little more than watch. Greg Vernouvage, a guide working with IMG, simply wrote on the team's blog later that he saw "the parapont guy fly off the summit of Everest, over the top of Nuptse, and apparently he went all the way to Syangboche (above Namche)!" He assumed it was Raineri flying solo, not knowing Babu and Lakpa were even on the mountain, let alone that they had intended to fly off of it. Ryan Waters and Sophie Denis, meanwhile, cheered Babu and Lakpa on from Camp II, descending after their successful summit of Lhotse. "I don't think they heard us, though," Waters says.

Babu's friend and expedition sponsor Kimberly Phinney watched a glowing yellow dot—representing their location—on her computer screen, live from her home in San Francisco. She hadn't heard anything from either Babu or Lakpa since they had departed from Kathmandu (in fact, she hadn't actually talked to Lakpa yet), but had stayed in contact with Arrufat, who had been talking to both Babu and Lakpa on the phone while they were in Base Camp waiting for the wing to arrive. He didn't have much information for her, though. She attempted to update the expedition website's blog for Babu as he and Lakpa went up the mountain, but the information she provided was sparse at best, based almost solely only the location of the little yellow dot on her screen that represented them. She wrote her blog posts in broken, misspelled English, as if Babu or Lakpa had been writing them.

The entirety of the expedition blog she posted on theultimate-descent.com, relating the team's two-month long ascent of Everest, read:

The Ultimate Descent 2011 "From highest place on Earth to the Sea"
Posted on March 31, 2011 by ruppy.kp
Welcome to our Blog
01/04/2011 Ultimate Descent Team
Posted on April 4, 2011 by ruppy.kp
Climbing team departs Kathmandu, headed towards Everest Base Camp
10/04/2011 Ultimate Descent Team
Posted on April 10, 2011 by ruppy.kp
Babu flying at Namche Bazar. Last village on the way to Base Camp
03/05/2011 Ultimate Descent Team
Posted on May 3, 2011 by ruppy.kp
Gps arrives at Base Camp.. Gps profile and live tracking, with link for whole trip log.
http://www.spotadventures.com/user/profile?user_id=69398
18/5/2011 5400m Ultimate Descent
Posted on May 18, 2011 by ruppy.kp
5:31:15am Everest Base Camp 5400m
Depart EBC for final rotation to summit . . .
18/5/2011 6500m Ultimate Descent Team
Posted on May 18, 2011 by ruppy.kp
5:16:50pm Camp 2 6500m
19/5/2011 7100m Ultimate Descent Team
Posted on May 19, 2011 by ruppy.kp
07:00:35 PM Camp 3 7100m
20/5/2011 7850m Ultimate Descent Team
Posted on May 20, 2011 by ruppy.kp

01:40:34 PM Camp 4
depart for summit at 09:24:56 PM
21/5/2011 8850m Ultimate Descent Team
Posted on May 21, 2011 by ruppy.kp
09:24:32 AM EVEREST SUMMIT, BEAUTIFUL BLUE
SKY, VERY SPECIAL DAY NAMASTE
21/5/2011 8850m Ultimate Descent Team
Posted on May 21, 2011 by ruppy.kp
09:44:57 AM TAKE OFF FROM EVEREST SUMMIT IN
TANDEM PARAGLIDER
SANO BABU SUNUWAR AND LAKPA CHHIRI SHERPA
WILL ATTEMPT TO MAKE HISTORY TODAY

When the yellow dot finally stopped moving on Phinney's screen at the Syangboche airstrip, a twelve-hour and forty-five-minute time difference away, at 11:34 p.m. in San Francisco on May 21 she posted:

21/5/2011 3750m Ultimate Descent Team
Posted on May 21, 2011 by ruppy.kp
10:49:52 AM Landed Namche Bazar, Syangboche Airstrip
After successful flying off the worlds highest mountain. Complet-
ing a 5000m descent 30k? XC PARAGLIDING FLIGHT OFF
THE SUMMIT OF EVEREST

That was it. The entire adventure summed up in 271 words.

Back on the summit, Babu and Lakpa's loyal but inexperienced sherpas, Ang Bhai and Nima Wang Chu, were left to walk back down the mountain on their own. Each had less than one full bottle of oxygen remaining. It was barely enough to make it down to Camp III, if they hurried. After watching their two friends get shot into the sky and then fly off to the south, they knew they couldn't loiter long on the summit. Nima quickly dug into his pack and began preparing his last bottle of oxygen. Ang Bhai, standing about 20 feet away from him on a cornice of snow overhanging the Kangshung Face where he had helped launch the wing, took a step forward and fell up to his waist into a narrow crevasse. The hole at his feet opened at the bottom to a clean 11,000-foot drop. He was afraid to move for fear of dislodging the thin layer of snow that was now the only thing keeping him from plummeting to his death.

"Nima!" he yelled. "NIMA!" But Nima, whose thick down hood was now cinched tight around his head to protect him from the ever-increasing icy wind, couldn't hear him. After about a minute, when he was done preparing his oxygen for the descent, he turned around and saw Ang Bhai stuck halfway into the crevasse. "Hold on!" Nima yelled, and without any hesitation he walked out onto the fractured cornice with his friend—unroped—grabbed his hand, and pulled him up.

Looking up, Ang Bhai saw that Babu and Lakpa were now nothing more than a small speck flying close to Nuptse. "I was feeling really lazy," Ang Bhai says. "I didn't think I could walk all the way down." Without another option, however, he and Nima both silently began their descent. It took three hours for them to reach Camp IV, where Nima, completely exhausted, collapsed into their tent and declared he couldn't go down any farther.

Without much discussion Ang Bhai left him half of the remaining food, asked him to bring the tent down with him the next day, and then continued down the mountain until he reached Camp II, carrying all six of the team's empty oxygen bottles, which had been left at Camp III. It was after 9:00 p.m., and at this point Ang Bhai had either been climbing or descending the mountain for nearly twenty-three hours straight. Unfortunately, Waters's team had already taken the tent Babu and Lakpa had borrowed from them back down to Base Camp earlier that day. "It was not so good for me," Ang Bhai points out. Fortunately, two other sherpas whom he had met earlier on the trip took pity on him and invited him to spend the night with them, sleeping head-to-toe, three of them wedged together in a two-person tent.

Nima spent the night alone at Camp IV, at 25,755 feet, without supplemental oxygen. A remarkable and decidedly dangerous accomplishment. He descended the next day and met Ang Bhai and Shri Hari in Base Camp. They then departed for Ang Bhai's parents' house just north of Namche Bazaar, where they hoped to reunite with Babu and Lakpa, assuming nothing horrible had happened to them during the flight.

⸺

After realizing that Babu and Lakpa had landed safely, David Arrufat, Wildes, Susmita, and Yanjee hopped on the first available flight to Lukla, in order to meet them before they continued their journey south to the sea. But not before David and Kimberly Phinney both sent e-mails to *Cross Country,* the world's largest paragliding and hang gliding magazine, based in Brighton, England, informing the editorial staff of Babu and Lakpa's achievement. Both promised photos soon.

Babu and Lakpa spent their first night celebrating their success with one of their friends, thirty-nine-year-old Ang Gyalgen Sherpa—the first Sherpa, coincidentally, to have started paragliding in the Khumbu a few years earlier—at a small bar just north of Namche Bazaar. Babu and Lakpa slept soundly that night, filled with beer, at Ang Bhai's parents' house nearby.

The next morning, they were promptly arrested by a Sagarmatha National Park ranger and taken to the park's main office in Namche Bazaar, where the army was waiting for them. The ranger had overheard Ang Bhai's father talking proudly about the expedition his son had just helped with at a public meeting the night before—while Babu, Lakpa, and Ang Gyalgen had been out drinking. And the ranger wasn't pleased.

"He asked us why we didn't have permits," Lakpa says. So Lakpa reminded him they didn't need a permit to climb Everest, because they were Sherpas, which was, at least for him, technically true. He didn't tell the ranger that Babu wasn't a Sherpa. The question of whether they needed a permit to actually fly off the mountain was a different matter. Was it an "obscene" record they had tried to set? Was it actually disrespectful to the mountain? There were no official, explicit rules written down saying they couldn't fly off of the summit of Everest, but the rangers apparently thought, in hindsight, that there probably should have been.

After thirty minutes of heated discussion, their friend Ang Gyalgen showed up. A wealthy, well-respected member of the community, he demanded their immediate release. Ang Gyalgen told them that Babu and Lakpa were trying to "open a new sport" in the region. "Trekking and climbing are too old-fashioned now," he told the army, perhaps referencing Lakpa's interest in one day taking his clients paragliding from other nearby summits, along with Everest. "So they did something new, so more people are going to come someday." It sounded like a noble cause, if not a realistic one. Word about their flight off of Everest was quickly spreading through the community, Ang Gyalgen also pointed out—Babu and Lakpa were on the fast track to becoming local celebrities. Perhaps the local people, he theorized, undoubtedly proud of their fellow Nepalis' accomplishment, might not like them being so hastily arrested after achieving it. This observation had a more profound effect. A few hours later, Babu and Lakpa were tentatively released, the park ranger and army major still confused as to what, exactly, Babu and Lakpa had done, why they had done it, or if they should actually be punished for it. They called their superiors in Kathmandu to ask their opinion.

Babu and Lakpa didn't wait around to find out the answer. They walked back toward Ang Bhai's parents' lodge laughing about their good fortune and met their friend Ryan Waters along the trail. He and Denis were just returning now from Base Camp, after summiting Lhotse. By flying down Babu and Lakpa had beat them back to Namche Bazaar by a full day.

"They were just happy, but not different," Waters says, recalling seeing them for the first time since their summit bid. "They were just their normal selves. It was like they pulled something off—like they got away with something, laughing about it." Waters joined Babu and Lakpa for a few Carlsburg beers at the teahouse back at the lodge, along with Lakpa's friend Tsering Nima, the owner of Himalayan Trailblazer, who had helped set up the logistics for their climb, as well as Shri Hari Shresthra, Ang Bhai, and Nima Wang Chu, who had all finally made it back down from Base Camp. "Everyone was successful," Waters says. "So everyone was in a good mood, having beers." They decided to walk to Lukla that night, all of them, together.

⌒‿⌒

Before they left, Lakpa and Babu hired a porter to trek with the paraglider and meet them in Lukla a full day after they left. "If anyone asks you about it," Lakpa said, "tell them it's a foreign trekker's." They weren't sure if they would have any more trouble with the military, so they decided it would be for the best if they didn't actually have any evidence of their flight off the mountain with them. It would be hard to explain away a paraglider if they were carrying one.

Babu and Lakpa walked to the south with the sun setting behind the mountains. The air was cool but not yet cold. They reached a high ridge in a canyon on the outskirts of the village where a wire suspension bridge crosses the Dudh Kosi. A group of soldiers was waiting for them. "They had guns," Lakpa says. The park ranger's superiors in Kathmandu weren't pleased with Babu and Lakpa's flight off Everest either and wanted them arrested again.

None of the soldiers assigned to bring them in had ever seen Babu or Lakpa before, however. Without the paraglider as evidence, and with every person in the Khumbu Valley being named after the day of the week on which they were born, the army had no way to be sure which Lakpa they were dealing with.

Sano Babu Sunuwar tests out the new ultralight wing, smuggled into the country from Malaysia, at Kala Patthar near Everest Base Camp.
BALKRISHNA BASEL

Nima Wang Chu (right) learns how to prepare the wing for takeoff from Sano Babu Sunuwar.
BALKRISHNA BASEL

Ryan Waters (left) does the math with Sano Babu Sunuwar to see if they'll actually clear the Northwest Ridge if he and Lakpa Tsheri Sherpa take off from the summit.
BALKRISHNA BASEL

Waters's base camp at the foot of the Khumbu Icefall.
BALKRISHNA BASEL

Lakpa Tsheri Sherpa (left) and Sano Babu Sunuwar pose with the Nepali flag at Everest Base Camp.
BALKRISHNA BASEL

Sano Babu Sunuwar, Lakpa Tsheri Sherpa, and Nima Wang Chu prepare the wing for takeoff on the Northeast Summit Ridge.
PHU DORJI SHERPA

Climbers cross a crevasse in the Western Cwm using aluminum ladders.
PHU DORJI SHERPA

Nima Wang Chu, one of the expedition's two sherpas.
BALKRISHNA BASEL

Phu Dorji, one of the expedition's two sherpas.
PHU DORJI SHERPA

Lakpa Tsheri Sherpa calls David Arrufat on his cellular phone from Everest Base Camp to check on the location of the team's paraglider.
BALKRISHNA BASEL

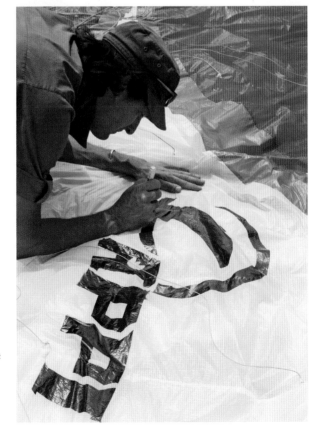

David Arrufat puts the APPI logo on Babu and Lakpa's paraglider in Pokhara.
BALKRISHNA BASEL

Shri Hari Shresthra (left), the team's cameraman, and Balkrishna Basel enter Sagarmatha National Park on their way to deliver the paraglider to Everest Base Camp.
BALKRISHNA BASEL

Balkrishna Basel holds the bag he smuggled the paraglider into Base Camp with, along with his clothes.
BALKRISHNA BASEL

Nima Wang Chu (left) watches as the team's cameraman, Shri Hari Shresthra (center), films Babu's inaugural flight with the new wing at Kala Patthar.
BALKRISHNA BASEL

The Sirkot headquarters of Babu and Lakpa's new paragliding company, Flying Himalayan.
DAVE COSTELLO

Lakpa Tsheri Sherpa on his Royal Enfield motorcycle in Pokhara.
DAVE COSTELLO

From left to right: Shri Hari Shresthra, Lakpa Tsheri Sherpa, Shailendra Kumar Upadhyay, and Sano Babu Sunuwar.
PHU DORJI SHERPA

Lakpa told Babu, "Let's go. Let's go. This is my place. We didn't kill any people, you know? We are not like robbers, you know? We keep going. This is my village. Let's go. Don't talk with them."

When they reached the bridge and the soldiers standing in front of it, they were asked to stop. "Why?" Lakpa asked. "What's the reason? Who gave you the authority to stop us?" The soldier was slow to respond and looked confused, as if the answer were obvious, and perhaps it was. "Give me a reason," Lakpa demanded again. "Any reason. We have to go farther. We have to be in India, not Nepal." At this, they kept walking. Leaving the soldiers befuddled behind them—and Shri Hari filming the whole exchange with his camera.

By the time Babu and Lakpa reached Lukla, almost everyone in the valley had heard about the two Nepalis who had flown off Everest. And they wanted to meet them. "When we got there, all the people started gathering because they had heard what Babu and Lakpa did," Waters said. "We had some beers and then those guys disappeared, because everyone wanted to talk with them." That was the last time Waters saw either Babu or Lakpa. He caught his flight back to Kathmandu early in the morning the next day, not knowing what would happen to them next.

That night, Babu and Lakpa reunited with their wives, as well as David and Wildes, all of whom were ecstatic to see them. Conversation was lively. The house was full and warm, everyone laughing, proud of what had just been accomplished.

❧

The Coupe Icare (Icarus Cup) is the world's largest paragliding and hang gliding festival, held each September in Saint-Hilaire, France; it includes the Free Flight International Film Festival. David and Wildes—who prefers to be called by her spiritual name, Mukti (meaning "one who brings liberation")—had plans to make a movie of the expedition, but it was going to be different than the movie Babu, Lakpa, and Shri Hari were working on. Unlike Babu and Lakpa's all-Nepali-made movie, David and Mukti's movie would be made by Westerners, for a Western audience, in time for the film festival.

"I pushed to do the movie, because I know if we do it in Nepal, it will never go out," David says, making the observation that most media produced within Nepal never leaves the country. "I made the movie for the festival, because I know they will not get it done in time. It would not fit with the standard of doing outside of Nepal. Shri Hari would make a good film, but it would not be what people want to see. We know what people want to see—people doing sport."

Babu and Lakpa still had to paraglide across the Himalaya and paddle to the ocean before Shri Hari would even begin working on editing the footage from their journey. And the Coupe Icare film submission deadline was only two months away.

So the morning after Babu and Lakpa's celebratory night, Mukti and David unpacked their own video cameras, gave Babu and Lakpa some more beer, and started recording. Mukti had a handwritten series of statements she had prepared the day before, which she now wanted Babu to say in front of the camera. "A script," she called it. "I am going to read for you. You tell me if you agree with what I am saying. If you agree, we speak about this. Then I turn on the camera, then you speak about this if you agree." Babu agreed.

"David and I are close to Babu," she explains. "I know Babu like a brother. And we share these feelings, and I know what is inside this story, and I try to put this in the movie, because the movie is giving emotion."

David pulled Babu aside while they were at Lakpa's parents' house. He told him that he wanted the photos from their cameras so he could get them to newspapers and magazines, to help promote their expedition. He also asked Babu to give him the memory cards from the GoPros they had used to film with while on the mountain, convincing him that submitting a short film to the Coupe Icare about just the climbing and flying portion of their expedition would be a good teaser for the full expedition film whenever it did come out.

"Babu came and stole two tapes from my home—of the flight," Lakpa says. "And used it without my permission, with his boss, David." Lakpa and Babu had both agreed before starting out that Lakpa would have all the film rights to the expedition and that Babu would have the rights to the still photos, which they hoped could eventually be sold to magazines.

In the yard, beneath a partly cloudy sky, Mukti helped Babu recite his lines before recording them with the camera. "Our goal is not only making summit," Babu repeated as best he could in his halting English, his face sunburned and peeling, his demeanor a little buzzed from the beer. "It is to see what's possible. Nobody has done it before. We want to show this."

———

Babu and Lakpa continued to evade national park authorities in Lukla for four more days, recovering from their climb and subsequent flight off Everest. On the fifth day they once again said good-bye to their family and friends. Their wives, along with David (carrying the memory cards containing the footage from their climb and flight), Mukti, and Shri Hari, boarded a plane at the Lukla airstrip back to Kathmandu. Later, Shri Hari would join the three-man Paddle Nepal support crew, who had driven nine hours to the capital from Pokhara and, at this point, supposedly had the team's kayak. The four men would then travel four hours north to Dolalghat, put in on the Sun Kosi River with Babu and Lakpa's kayak strapped to the back of the support raft, and paddle downstream approximately 20 miles of Class II-IV whitewater. If everything went according to plan, Babu and Lakpa would be waiting for them on the riverbank somewhere near the confluence of the Dudh Kosi.

The fact that the Paddle Nepal support crew actually had a shiny new 12-foot, 1-inch orange tandem whitewater kayak in their possession was a bit of a miracle. Babu's friend Pete Astles, back in the United Kingdom, had ordered the kayak directly from the Jackson

Kayak factory in Tennessee. It was then flown, via a standard commercial passenger jet, to Tribhuvan International Airport in Kathmandu, under someone else's name. It had been the only even remotely feasible way to get the $1,500 boat, which was barely within the length restrictions for the plane, into the country on such short notice. It was also the most difficult way to get such a large, obvious, big-ticket item through Nepali customs.

"If you bring any foreign goods into Nepal, the customs department is very difficult to deal with," Mahendra Singh Thapa, Babu and Astles's mutual friend and owner of the Kathmandu-based outfitter Equator Expeditions, says. "Importing anything in Nepal is very tricky. Taxes and customs for foreign goods cost almost 200 percent. I know how to deal with customs, because I'm importing goods all the time. So I told Pete, 'OK, you send the kayak in my name, and I will deal with the customs.'" Thapa, a strong, deep-chested man whose outfitter is one of the largest and oldest in the country, walked out of the airport with the kayak (as well as all of the additional paddling gear Astles had stuffed inside of it), having paid some money, but not in taxes. And it wasn't nearly 200 percent of the retail price of the boat.

From there, Thapa put the bright yellow kayak on a truck along with the Paddle Nepal support raft and wished good luck to the three-man crew, which consisted of two of Babu's good raft-guiding friends, Madhukar Pahari and Resham Bahadur Thapa, and his younger brother, Krishna. All of whom had volunteered their time, without pay, to help Babu and Lakpa down the river portion of their journey. The trio picked up cameraman Shri Hari and headed north, into the mountains. Four hours later, as they put on the river at Dolalghat, they still had no idea whether Babu and Lakpa would actually show up at their designated rendezvous point just south of the Dudh Kosi confluence 20 miles downstream. There was no Plan B if they didn't. They strapped the tandem kayak onto the back of their raft anyway and shoved off the riverbank.

———

Babu and Lakpa walked together south, back toward Lakpa's parents' home in Chaurikharka, where they spent the night. The next morning they picked up their paraglider, still hidden in its black backpack, and continued walking the trail south along the Dudh Kosi, just under two hours to the small mountain village of Kharte, climbing to the top of a western-facing ridge just to the north of town. The two men stopped on a small, grassy clearing overlooking the river several hundred feet below and unpacked their wing. They looked south. The mountains were no longer white and black, covered in ice, snow, and rock, but a dense green now, covered in either rice terraces or dark, leafy jungle. Smaller in scale, less jagged, but more remote and isolated. According to their GPS track log, they were at an elevation of approximately 10,100 feet, nearly 19,000 feet lower than they had been just a week earlier.

Babu and Lakpa had no tent, no provisions. Nothing but the clothes on their backs, the shoes on their feet, and their paraglider. Babu and Lakpa also had no map, and the goal of landing within the week on a small sandbar on a remote mountain river that was still over 40 miles away. In front of them was a series of deep gorges and canyons no one had ever previously thought to pilot a paraglider through.

Making exploratory cross-country flights with inexperienced cohorts was not an entirely new challenge to Babu. Just the year before, he had flown a tandem paraglider across Nepal from west to east with Shri Hari, who, like Lakpa, didn't know how to fly. They had started in the town of Baitadi on Nepal's western border with India, along with seventeen other pilots—mostly foreign—all looking to become the first to make the crossing. No one had ever done it before. After thirty days, two canopy collapses, and one backward landing, they were the only team to successfully arrive on the eastern border of the country. They had spent eighteen days actually flying. The rest had been spent walking, often not on roads. Up and down remote mountain valleys, looking for the next suitable ridgeline to launch from. Every other team had abandoned their crossing along the way. One got stuck dangling in a tree for twenty-four hours. Babu had used a second-hand tandem wing, which had been given to him by Mukti. With both Babu and Shri Hari and his camera gear attached, they nearly maxed out the 396-pound weight limit, so they couldn't carry any additional supplies, like a tent, or more than a day's worth of food.

"It answered the question, 'What's my country like?'" Babu later told a reporter for *Action Asia* magazine, referring to his trans-Nepal flight. "There are so many things that have to be done, roads, education, political system and so on. It's the only way to see Nepal and it's many different cultures and castes." The experience also made a bit of a politico out of him. After seeing his country Babu wanted to change it. And he recognized that the only reason he got his name in a magazine, and had the opportunity to share his opinions and insights with the rest of the world, was that he had done something construed as crazy by the majority of the population.

Lakpa, now done with his end of the bargain—getting them to the top of Everest—was happy, singing as he helped Babu unfold their new wing for its second flight into the unknown. Or third, since they had first unwrapped it at Kala Patthar. Babu inflated the 51-foot-wide sheet of red and white nylon into the light breeze that was blowing and launched them over the valley. To anyone below they appeared to be an upside-down bright red crescent drifting slowly through the mountains, a single speck hanging beneath it from string. The flight itself was uneventful, and unremarkable other than the fact that it didn't last long. In less than twenty minutes, they were on the ground, on the other side of the mountains that ran to the east, in a different river drainage, the Inkhu Kosi. They were nowhere near the only foot-path leading anywhere, which was on the other side of the mountains running along the Dudh Kosi.

Like he had done so many times on his cross-Nepal expedition the year before, Babu packed up the paraglider, put it on his back, and started walking south. Bushwhacking his way through the jungle, he looked for a place to relaunch. Lakpa followed. After six hours they reached the hillside village of Waku, near where the Inkhu Kosi and Dudh Kosi converge in a slight widening of the Dudh Kosi River gorge. They hadn't eaten all day. Lakpa gave a few rupees to a local farm family in exchange for a place to sleep that night in their home, as well as a meal of dal bhat. Exhausted and grateful for shelter, the two men slept in the company of the family's chickens.

The next morning, it was determined that there were no suitable places to launch a paraglider nearby, the surrounding hillsides too steep and forested to provide a proper, or even remotely safe, takeoff. So Babu and Lakpa thanked their host family and continued walking along the only footpath south, four hours to the similarly picturesque mountaintop village of Deurali—a small collection of gray stone buildings hugging the steep, rolling, perpetually terraced hillsides. White clouds floated above and below.

It was here that their SPOT locator stopped working. Back in Pokhara and in San Francisco, the little yellow dot on both the Arrufats' and Phinney's computer screens wasn't moving again. And it didn't move for four days. Neither Lakpa nor Babu had thought to change the GPS batteries.

A few days earlier, Phinney had posted on the blog again:

22/5/2011- 28/5/2011 2050m Ultimate Descent Team
Posted on May 28, 2011 by ruppy.kp
Hike and Fly to Koshi river, see our Gps log for tracking..

Now there was no way to track them or their progress, or lack thereof. Phinney had absolutely no idea what was going on with the expedition anymore and was afraid for her friends' lives. David Arrufat, meanwhile, had posted a blog of his own on APPIfly.org, his paragliding organization's website, which a few days later would feature screen grabs and photos from the two memory cards Babu had given him, with the APPI logo and website URL embedded as a watermark.

APPI Tandem Pilot Sano Babu Sunuwar took off from the summit of Everest with Sherpa Lapka flying over the world's highest mountain!!!

Babu, a twenty-eight years old APPI Tandem Pilot, has successfully flown with a paraglider over the summit of Everest today, May 21st 2011. He had the most incredible flight ever done and broken the record of height and distance. Babu gained altitude over the take off, at the summit of Mt. Everest, and had a 31km cross-country flight over the biggest mountains of the world.

Landing at the airport of Namche Bazaar, the Sherpa town and mountain capital of the Everest region, at an altitude of 3,750m, Babu now is getting ready to continue his adventure, by kayak Topolino/duo, from Nepal, crossing to India, and to a final arrival in the ocean, in Bangladesh.

Babu has flown on tandem with his passenger Lakpa Tshering Sherpa, 35-year-old, an experienced Everest man, who had reached the summit several times on the past years—and is going to continue the adventure on the river, as well—even if he doesn't know how to swim. Lakpa Sherpa does not stop his challenges there, trusting Babu with his river guide experience.

Babu and Lakpa, with a camera man and a cooker man, climbed together Everest from the Nepal side along the classic South Col route. They took off from the north-west side of Everest, following the ridge down to the other side to the Western Ridge and into the Everest basin.

From there to the south-west, crossing the massive Nuptse of 7,861m, continuing in a straight line, crossing the summit of Pokalde Peak at 5,806m, popular trekking route, to Ama Dablam, and finally arriving—nothing better to land than a simple mountain airport, if we can say so—at the airstrip of Syangboche.

Babu, full name Sano babu Sunuwar, is an APPI tandem pilot, certified at an APPI paragliding school in Nepal. He has been trained by David Arrufat and sponsored by APPI for his challenging character, optimism and inner determination.

What we could say about Babu is that he is a lucky man and beloved one who always have something positive to say, if not an smile to give. Here is Babu full power smile at the Base Camp, before the ascent to the flight which would make him a legend.

On March 2010, Babu completed his previous challenge of crossing his home country in tandem bivouac, in a 850km 30-day adventure from east to west of Nepal. Where Babu has seen incredible contrasts of his country on beauty, simplicity and lots of adrenaline, with thermals more than 18m/s, and having Shree Shestra as his passenger and camera man.

Having so much love for nature, rivers and mountains, Babu named his second son of four months old, nothing less than "Himalaya", as soon as the baby was born – on the time that he had no plan yet to fly from Everest, even if it was an old dream since he started to fly. The idea came just little after, when once again he met his friend Lakpa and decided that he had found the right person as a passenger, partner and brother for a life story.

The day after they had flown off the mountain, *Cross Country* also posted a short story on its website, titled "Babu Sunuwar Flies Off Everest," based on information Arrufat supplied them. The news of Lakpa and Babu's Everest flight was getting out. And Lakpa, unknowingly, was turning into a footnote.

~

With no way to communicate with Arrufat, Phinney, or anyone else in the outside world, Babu and Lakpa continued their journey south toward the Sun Kosi River. They launched from a rice paddy in Deurali and flew over the ridgeline village of Aiselukharka, down into the next valley, where they unceremoniously landed in the trees. After untangling their wing, Babu and Lakpa hiked thirty minutes to the nearest village, Rawa Khola, where the two friends jumped in the nearby river to bathe. To celebrate, they drank prodigious amounts of *chhaang* ("nectar of the gods"), a locally made grain alcohol similar to unfiltered rice wine. They stumbled up the ridge to the south of town, aiming to launch off the top of it that night, but didn't make it. Instead, they opted to lie down on the ground on the hillside in the forest and sleep off the chhaang.

From the ridgeline the next morning, it was a ten-minute flight down to the small hilltop Sherpa city of Lamidanda. With a population of over 2,000, it has an airport but no roads, just heavily worn dirt footpaths. The roofs of the nicer stone buildings are covered in corrugated aluminum, either hiked in from the nearest road, which is nearly 15 miles away, or flown in from Kathmandu. Babu called his friend Nim Magar at Paddle Nepal to see where the kayak, the support crew, and Shri Hari were. They were a day behind, Magar told him. He and Lakpa could expect to meet their kayak and support crew at the rendezvous point just to the south of the confluence of the Dudh Kosi and Sun Kosi in three days.

Lakpa bought batteries for their SPOT locator but didn't turn it on. He then called his sister, Ang Maya in Kathmandu, from a payphone and asked her to wire him some money. "I brought 50,000 rupees [about $500] from Lukla," Lakpa says. "And that was not enough." Without Babu being able to pay for any of their expenses, Lakpa had already managed to burn through his trip cash, paying for their room and board, as well as all the chhaang at the villages they had stopped at along the way. Ang Maya agreed to wire him 5,000 rupees for the rest of the trip, about $50.

After getting the cash from the local bank, they continued walking on the footpath south to Halesi Mahadev, a sacred cave and Buddhist temple tucked into the hills five hours away. The cave itself is a quiet, dimly lit sanctuary with trees growing up straight out of the sides of the rock-wall entrance and steps carved right into the bedrock, leading down into the cave. They spent two nights talking and praying with the red-robed monks, flying off a nearby ridge for fun during the day. They flew off the same ridge again the third morning, covering only a few miles before crash landing in a cluster of rhododendron trees. When they finally managed to untangle themselves from the branches, Lakpa felt a sharp pain in his right knee. It hurt to walk. Their $4,000 wing also looked worse for wear. A series of holes was now clearly visible in the fabric—some of them quite large. They decided between them that, in spite of the damage, it would probably be "fine" to fly it one more day.

Babu and Lakpa hiked up the final ridge before the river and rested, camping out under the stars and a waning moon on a hilltop without having any dal bhat. The next morning came without break-fast, and they launched their damaged wing at 10:00 a.m. in the hopes of spotting their support crew floating down the river to meet them with a kayak, and hopefully more food.

After an hour of riding thermals—upward-flowing columns of air that help keep paragliders aloft in the sky—there was no support raft to be seen. Just green mountains beneath a blue sky and a massive, brown surging river.

VIII

River of Gold

Sidi, Nepal,
June 2011—Approximately 2,900 Feet

Hamilton Pevec sat alone on a futon in a small room just north of Pokhara in the small village of Sidi, surrounded by four short walls made of stacked whitewashed fieldstone. The cement floor felt cold against his feet. Light filtered through a single paneless window and an open, doorless doorway, illuminating the white smoke rising from the lit joint in his hand. Outside, Arrufat's chickens clucked and a lone rooster named Coco crowed. David and Mukti's three-year-old daughter, Yada, ran after him, laughing. The bird was as tall as she was, the guest observed, looking out the empty window.

Pevec, a twenty-eight-year-old documentary filmmaker from Carbondale, Colorado, stood up from the old personal computer the Arrufats had bought and subsequently brought into their home for him to work on, walked over to the doorway, and chased a curious hen that had wandered into the room back into the yard. He was busy and stressed, preoccupied with reviewing the hours of video footage the Arrufats had just given him from Babu and Lakpa's recent flight off Everest, but he wasn't about to let chickens start crapping on the floor of his new editing suite. He had a movie to make, and not much time to make it.

A slow talker with a short, well-kept beard and a neck-length black ponytail, Pevec had been coming to Nepal since 2007, when he had fallen in love with a thirty-year-old Nepali yoga instructor named Devika Gurumg. He had moved from his home in Colorado to Dharamsala, India, where he spent several months instructing the Dalai Lama's monks on modern video production techniques, working as a volunteer for the Namgyal Monastery Audio Visual Archive Center.*

"I was living at the monastery," Pevec says. "Devika and I had a mutual friend, and she invited me to Devika's yoga studio in Pokhara. I fell in love with her. We had this on-again, off-again relationship over a couple of years. Then I promised I would be back in 2011. So I went back to see if our relationship was still alive and well, and sure enough, it was. And I fell in love with her all over again."

Gurumg, a beautiful, brown-eyed woman with long, dark hair, was one of six children. She had spent her childhood picking fruit in orchards, making carpets, and housekeeping, until two Australian women took it upon themselves to teach her Hatha Yoga twice a day, every day, for three months. She was eighteen. By the time Pevec met her, she was running her own yoga studio in Pokhara. By 2011, when her and Pevec's love was rekindled, she had become good friends with the Arrufats. She introduced Hamilton to David and Mukti, who had just started their new for-profit paragliding organization, the Association of Paragliding Pilots and Instructors, the year before, in 2010.

"They offered me a proposition," Pevec says. "They said, 'We'll teach Devika to fly if you make us some promo stuff for APPI, because we want to launch APPI.'" Pevec thought it was a fair trade, so he agreed. "I started shooting this promotional video for APPI," he says, "and Devika started learning how to fly, and about a week into shooting

---

* The Namgyal Monastery Audio Visual Archive Center's sole purpose is recording the Dalai Lama's teachings through both audio and video. It was founded in 1980 and originally operated by the Meridian Trust, a UK-based nonprofit that looks to preserve Tibet's cultural heritage. The program was taken over by the Namgyal Monastery itself after the trust suddenly took all of its camera equipment back in 1989. Now filmmakers from around the world volunteer their time, helping the monks themselves record His Holiness's teachings.

these interviews with pilots and stuff, Babu and Lakpa launched their paraglider off the summit." He had no idea who Babu and Lakpa even were at the time. "That changed everything," he says. "Immediately, David and Mukti went up there to meet them. A few days later they came back with the footage, handed it to me, and said, 'Stop what you are doing and turn this into a movie.'" Awestruck by the opportunity to make a movie about someone flying off the top of Everest, rather than a low-budget promo video, Pevec agreed, in spite of the fact that it would require significantly more work on his part.

"Using it as a promotional device to launch APPI was part of the plan," Pevec says. He didn't know about Lakpa, Babu, and Shri Hari's plan to make their own movie of the expedition.

David and Mukti bought a computer that was several years old, carried it up the narrow, rocky creek drainage that served as their driveway, and placed it in the back room of the single-story stone house they were renting in Sidi, just a few miles north of Lakeside. Pevec downloaded pirated editing software onto the computer's hard drive and started reviewing Babu and Lakpa's footage from the mountain, whenever the electricity was working. "We only had electricity for a few hours a day," Pevec says. "We never knew when it was coming on or going off." They purchased a large battery that had enough juice to keep the computer running just long enough after the power went out for Pevec to save his edits before the computer would shut off completely. "It was a technical nightmare," he says. David loaned Pevec his bicycle, which he used to ride to and from Devika's place in Pokhara to the Arrufats' each day. "He handed me this big jar of weed," Pevec recalls. "Said, 'This will help you get through it.' And sure enough, that was the fuel for the film." He started working twelve-hour days, every day, in order to make the July 15 deadline for the Coupe Icare festival, less than two months away.

The footage itself was rough at best. "Mukti shot the interviews when they were both really drunk," Pevec says. "Babu and Lakpa were pretty wasted." The rest was shaky, handheld GoPro footage. "I didn't get anything that the other filmmaker got," Pevec says, referring to Shri Hari, not realizing the reason why he didn't have any of the footage.

He didn't have permission to use it.

— · —

Krishna Sunuwar looked up between the green hills rising from the Sun Kosi River at a clear blue sky, scanning the elevated horizon line for his older brother. The sandy beach where Babu and Lakpa were supposed to be waiting to meet them was empty. He knew they must still be in flight, or still walking to the river, which was now swollen and orange-brown with the recent heavy monsoon rains. Paddling a red 8-foot Riot brand whitewater kayak built in the early 2000s, which was loaned to him by his boss, Charley Gaillard, owner of the Ganesh Kayak Shop, Krishna kept his neck craned upward, squinting into the sun. He also kept a paddle blade poised over the fast-moving water beside him, wrist cocked forward, ready to brace himself in the case of an unexpected surge of the current.

Next to him, in a large blue raft emblazoned with a Paddle Nepal logo, sat Babu and Lakpa's bespectacled cameraman, Shri Hari, as well as his and Babu's mutual friends and fellow raft guides, Madhukar Pahari and Resham Bahadur Thapa. Both had been sent by Nim and Kelly Magar, along with the raft Madhukar was rowing, from Paddle Nepal back in Pokhara. They had been on the river for three days. The raft itself was equipped with two large oars attached to an aluminum frame and enough food to feed six people for another three days. Just enough time to reach their takeout at Chatra, near the Indian border: the end of the Sun Kosi's steep whitewater, and the start of the grid-iron-flat Gangetic Plain, where Babu, Lakpa, and Krishna would continue their journey south through India to the Bay of Bengal. A shiny new tandem kayak was strapped on the back of the raft, its rounded orange hull facing up to the sky. It was still wrapped in plastic.

Krishna, who had taken over Babu's old job at the Ganesh Kayak Shop in Pokhara when his older brother had switched over to working for David Arrufat at Blue Sky Paragliding, had volunteered to paddle with Babu and Lakpa all the way to the ocean, without pay. He knew that Lakpa, whom he had met only a handful of times over the past few months, couldn't swim and had never paddled before in his life. Krishna's job, Babu had told him before they had left for Everest, was to save Lakpa if they capsized. That was it.

A slightly younger and even shorter, stockier version of Babu, Krishna had also taken to the water like a fish after leaving their village. In the same amount of time it had taken his brother to become an expert paragliding pilot (about two years), Krishna had become an expert kayaker, regularly paddling Class V rapids all over Nepal with his brother. And he was equally prone to taking significant risks. The year before, he had paddled the Sun Kosi for the first time. Solo. In a boat he had borrowed from Gaillard. The reason, he explains, was so that he could visit his family back in Rampur-6, paddling 170 miles of Class III-IV high-volume whitewater, completely alone, so that he could say hello to his mother, whom he hadn't seen in a year.

As Krishna was about to land on the beach where he, Madhukar, and Resham were supposed to meet Babu and Lakpa, Krishna saw the red crescent of a paraglider rise over the ridgeline to his left. He watched it circle over the swirling river above their heads and land, his brother and Lakpa dangling beneath it. They touched down on the beach just in front of the raft. Both of them were smiling broadly and laughing, celebrating the fact that the flying portion of their journey was now over.

After a short, happy greeting, Krishna went to work setting up camp, preparing a meal of dal bhat and erecting the two tents they had among the six of them on the sand. Babu and Lakpa, meanwhile, unloaded the bright orange tandem kayak that was strapped to the back of the support raft and removed it from its plastic packaging. Inside, they found two new Peak UK PFDs, two new paddles, two new drytops, and two new neoprene spray skirts, which they would have to wear around their waists and attach to the combing around the kayak's two cockpits in order to keep water out of the boat while they were paddling it. Madhukar and Resham had brought them each a blue cotton T-shirt sporting the Paddle Nepal logo. The plan was for them to wear the same helmets on the river that they had been wearing on Everest and on their recent cross-country flight. Pete Astles had shipped them everything else they needed from the United Kingdom, free of charge.

They laid the gear out on the ground. Lakpa stared at it, then looked at the frothing brown river beside him, then back at the gear laid out on the sand, and then at the narrow, long, log-looking kayak at his feet. He imagined himself sitting inside of it, along with Babu, floating on the swollen brown river, bobbing out of control beyond the next bend wrapping around the green-covered mountains in front of him. He imagined what was beyond that bend. He then looked at Babu and said, "I can't do this."

After some discussion the group convinced Lakpa, who had never been on a river before, to get in the raft with Madhukar. They pushed off from the beach into a large, flat eddy and paddled the blue inflatable in circles for a few minutes. Lakpa, looking anxiously over the sides of the raft, waited to see what, if anything, would happen to him. Nothing did. The sun dropped behind the mountains to the west.

"He was scared of the water," Shri Hari says. "Only after Lakpa gained some confidence in the raft did he agree to get in the kayak with Babu."

That same evening, Lakpa clambered into the front seat of the kayak, Babu sitting behind him. He didn't like the idea of being trapped inside the small boat, upside down in the water, so he and Babu pushed off into the calm eddy in front of their camp not wearing their spray skirts. Babu showed him how to hold the paddle, the slight concave shape in the blade facing toward him, and proceeded to go around in small circles, alternating between turning to the right and to the left until dark. It was the first time Lakpa had ever touched a paddle or sat in a kayak, and it was the only preparation he would have before setting off on their journey to the ocean, starting with the Class IV big-water rapids that Babu and Krishna knew were only a few miles downstream.

Babu had never paddled a tandem kayak before, let alone with someone who didn't know how to paddle to begin with, and he wondered—if they did flip—whether he could even roll it back upright.

───

Rising in Tibet from a series of small, snow-fed streams at the base of the 26,289-foot Gosainthan Massif, the headwater of the Sun Kosi River is referred to locally as the Matsang Tsangpo. The river, which starts as a simple meandering white-gray creek tumbling between snowcapped mountains, picks up speed and volume as it cuts south through the Himalaya at the bottom of a deep, cavernous gorge. Intersected by numerous feeder creeks, its water level slowly rises, boring its way through the heart of the Himalaya. Unannounced, the river's name changes suddenly upon crossing an imaginary line delineating the border between Tibet and Nepal. Once in Nepal, the river is no longer referred to as the Matsang Tsangpo, but rather as the Sun Kosi—"the River of Gold," the word *sun* in Nepali meaning "gold." * The newly renamed river continues to flow south, joined by the nearby Bhote Kosi just downstream of Barabise, gaining even more water until reaching its confluence with the Indrawati Nadi, which dumps into it from the northwest at Dolalghat, nearly doubling its volume. This is where most commercial raft trips on the river choose to begin, and it is where Krishna, Shri Hari, and the Paddle Nepal support crew started paddling downstream to meet Babu and Lakpa.

At Dolalghat the Sun Kosi turns gradually to the southeast, flowing through a wide, deep valley separating the slightly lower,

---

* The "River of Gold" gets its name either from the small flecks of gold that are sometimes panned out of its gravel beds or from the orange-brown color of its waters during the monsoon, when the entire length of the Sun Kosi runs thick and dark with alluvial silt. Likely, the name originated with a little bit of help from both of these attributes.

green-covered Mahabharat Mountains to the south and the high, white-crested Himalaya to the north. Over the next 175 miles, it drops an average of 10 feet per mile until finally reaching Chatra and the start of the Gangetic Plain, where it flows steadily, if not more slowly, onward toward the sea through India, where it eventually merges with the holy Ganges. As it pours through the valley between the Mahabharat Mountains and the Himalaya, the river meets with myriad other tributaries emptying down into it from high in the mountains, primarily from the north, including the Tamba Kosi, Likhu Khola, Majhigau Khola, and Dudh Kosi, along with the Arun and Tamur, eventually, near Chatra. Thus draining the majority of eastern Nepal.

The amount of water in the Sun Kosi increases considerably with the flow from these tributaries. In November, the dry season in Nepal, the amount of water in the Sun Kosi moving past any given point along its banks at Dolalghat is about 3,500 cubic feet per second (cfs)—enough to fill an Olympic-size swimming pool approximately every twenty-five seconds. Just over 50 miles downstream, where Babu and Lakpa's team was about to put in, just below the Dudh Kosi confluence, it's approximately 11,000 cfs—a typical flow for the Grand Canyon of the Colorado. Just a little farther on, at Chatra, after the Arun and Tamur confluences, the flow is regularly over 28,000 cfs. And that's when the Sun Kosi is low.

Starting with the onset of the monsoon rains in June, when Lakpa, Babu, and their team were putting into the river, flows just below the Dudh Kosi confluence often jump to over 21,000 cfs within a matter of days. Each individual drop of water falling from the sky combines with the ones next to it, slowly flowing downhill to meet with others, until finally they become a massive wall of tumultuous whitewater. By July there's typically more than 100,000 cfs flowing past the same spot—enough to fill nearly two and a half Olympic-size swimming pools in two seconds. At these levels small ripples turn into 10-foot standing waves followed by recirculating holes large enough to swallow a bus.

Whirlpools form in eddies capable of consuming and submerging an entire kayak. Paddler included.

And that's not to mention the continual threat of a glacial lake outburst flood (GLOF): in short, an entire glacial lake emptying into a river drainage at the drop of a hat. And it happens with some regularity all across the Himalaya, about once or twice every decade, give or take. It occurs after a large, semisolid geological feature, such as a glacial moraine constructed of loosely consolidated stones and ice, suddenly bursts from the pressure created by the thousands upon thousands of tons of glacial meltwater that has been collecting behind it for years, sometimes centuries. This, in effect, unleashes hell.

In 1998 Manish Rai, a Nepali raft guide trainee of the same caste as Babu, was paddling a commercial group's gear raft downstream just north of the Dudh Kosi confluence, near the same spot on the Sun Kosi that Babu and Lakpa were now standing, when a GLOF hit, pouring down from the Dudh Kosi drainage. In an interview with Peter Knowles, author of the guidebook *White Water Nepal*, he later said, "It was as if we were paddling uphill. As if the river was backing up . . . the water was like liquid mud, chocolate brown color and there were big trees and the remains of houses being tossed around and swirling in the current." Within twenty seconds two of the three rafts in his group flipped, including the one Manish was rowing.

Manish managed to clamber back on top of the raft, which was miraculously flipped back upright amidst the swirling chaos, but was flushed downstream, alone, after discovering one of the oarlocks—the part of the rowing frame that attaches to the oar itself—had been sheared clean off. The rest of the group made it to shore. Two safety kayakers took after him. One pulled out a mile downstream, fearing for his life. The other, a Nepali named Tarka Kumal, continued his pursuit.

"I saw my friend Tarka and I cried for him," Manish told Knowles. "I shouted, 'Please don't follow me! Please don't follow me!' I felt that I would probably die, but I did not want my friend to die with me."

Swimming to shore wasn't an option. "This seemed certain death," Manish went on to say. "There was no flat water—just huge waves and sometimes we crashed into a tree or a log. The water was this horrible brown color, there were masses of dead fish floating on the surface and I then saw Tarka hit and capsized by a huge log and I lost sight of him."

The raft Manish was in continued to capsize, repeatedly. "I thought that it would never end," he says. "I had given up hope and just prayed to my gods." He and Tarka were eventually pulled out of the river, half-drowned, several miles farther downstream by villagers. Manish's eyes and nose were completely blocked by mud. After washing them out, he realized that he had also lost his shorts in the fray. He had been stripped naked by the force of the water. They were evacuated by helicopter a few days later.

The sun rose slowly behind the hills to the west of the gravel bar where Lakpa, Babu, and their support team were camped. The sky was a crisp blue framed against the valley below: a long, green shadow with a dark, churning white-orange river pushing through it. The air was cool but not cold. It was to be Lakpa's second day of kayaking, the start of a 300-plus-mile paddle to the Bay of Bengal. As Krishna prepared breakfast on a small gas stove, Lakpa asked Babu for the names of the first rapids they were going to encounter that day.

"Jaws," Babu says. "And Dead Man's Eddy."

Lakpa proceeded to put on his gear, his spray skirt first, stepping into it just like he would an actual skirt, as Babu had shown him the day before. Sand stuck to the edges of the oval-shaped neoprene, which was still wet with dew from the night before. Then he pulled his PFD over his head and cinched down the two buckles on each side, so that it would cinch-shut the top of the spray skirt's neoprene tunnel that was around his waist, which would help keep more water out of the boat. This Babu had also shown him the day before, after they had practiced paddling in the calm eddy next to their camp. Lakpa then put on his blue skateboard helmet with the Nepali flag sticker, which he had worn on Everest, picked up his paddle, and wedged himself legs first into the front cockpit of the tandem kayak. The balls of his feet touched the adjustable bulkhead in front of him, which Babu had set in place for him the day before, making sure that Lakpa's thighs were pressed firmly against the concave foam-padded thigh braces located just under the cockpit combing once it was set. This, he told Lakpa, was so that he could use his lower body to adjust the tilt of the boat in the water. Why, exactly, he would want to do that, Lakpa had absolutely no idea.

Pete Astles, Babu's friend and paddling mentor who shipped the tandem kayak, has paddled the Sun Kosi from Dolalghat to Chatra three times. He describes Dead Man's Eddy like this: "The river goes to a right-angle bend. There's a huge cliff, and it creates a massive eddy line, just a real swirling whirlpool. All sorts of stuff gets caught in there." The "stuff" he's referring to often includes dead human bodies, hence the rapid's name. As a part of local tradition, the bodies of the deceased are regularly put in the river, which is considered holy and, in general, a good place to be if you're dead. These bodies, like all other floating things in the river, eventually get caught in the recirculating currents found in eddies along the riverbank, where water moving downstream is forced back up to fill a hole created by an obstruction in the current. Dead Man's Eddy is one of the largest and strongest of these features on the Sun Kosi. Placed along a sharp right angle in the river, the water hits a massive headwall, creating a nearly river-wide whirlpool. Half the current goes right, downstream; half goes left, back up against the cliff. The left side is more than capable of holding a kayak, raft, or human body—live or dead—within its vortex for an extended period of time. At lower water it's a manageable Class II maneuver to avoid it. At high water it's deadly.

Nim Magar, a co-owner of Paddle Nepal, the company that supplied the support raft and crew, and one of Babu's best friends, has paddled the Sun Kosi more times than he can remember. He has guided the run commercially for years. "We always scout Dead Man's Eddy," he says. "At some water levels, we can sneak around to the right." Otherwise, he and his guides always make their clients walk around. "It looks simple," he says, "but if you get in there, it's too difficult to get out. Lots of people have died there. You can't cross swimming in the main current. You'd go around and around and around. . . . We don't want to see a customer go in there. Even if we go in there, we can't get out."

He had warned Babu about Dead Man's Eddy and asked him not to run it, knowing that the water would likely be at a medium to medium-high flow. "I told Babu, 'You guys need to run safe lines,'" Magar says. He would send his gear and staff only if Babu and Lakpa promised to not run "crazy rapids." Dead Man's Eddy was one of these crazy rapids, the craziest at medium-high water, in Magar's opinion. "You do it on the safe side," he told Babu. "And they said OK," he recalls.

Before Dead Man's Eddy, however, there was Jaws to deal with first: a difficult, long Class IV wave train littered with massive holes capable of flipping a 16-foot raft like a pancake. Most of these holes are stacked near the top of the rapid. Only a few hundred feet separate the run-out of Jaws and the lead-in to Dead Man's Eddy. A single, large eddy is on river right,* where Babu and Lakpa would need to be if they wanted to avoid going into the massive whirlpool on river left. It's easy to hit if you're in your boat and in control. It's not if you're swimming. The majority of the current feeds left, toward Dead Man's Eddy.

In October 1999, during a period of high flow on the Sun Kosi (over 50,000 cfs), an experienced forty-four-year-old kayaker named Jim Traverso flipped amidst the large exploding waves that make up Jaws. A fellow kayaker in the group managed to reach him but was

---

* Since the right and left side of a river can switch depending on what direction you're facing, paddlers typically use the terms "river right" and "river left" to describe directions in relation to facing downstream. This is similar to how actors use the directions "stage right" and "stage left."

unable to pull him to shore before a huge surge of water separated them just above Dead Man's Eddy, pushing Traverso left, into Dead Man's, and his rescuer right, to safety. It was the last time Traverso was seen alive. All of his team members' efforts to retrieve him failed, including an attempt at paddling into the recirculating eddy themselves, as well as descending the cliff from above. The accident report filed with American Whitewater soon after the incident stated:

The rescuers found Jim floating face down. His skin was gray and his eyes open. His helmet was still on, and there was no visible sign of injury. Two kayakers entered the eddy and tried to push Jim to shore. They were unsuccessful and quickly became exhausted. As they prepared for a second attempt, Jim's life jacket was pulled from his body. After a few brief moments near the surface he disappeared under water.

His body was never found.

Babu knew that Jaws probably wouldn't be a good place for Lakpa to learn how to swim. Just in case, however, he proceeded to instruct his friend on the finer points of surviving a rapid outside of a kayak, before they actually pushed off from shore that first morning into the mouth of Jaws. The general strategy is to lay on your back, not entirely unlike a sea otter, with your feet up in front of you, facing downstream, and to back paddle with both your arms at an angle slightly against the current so that you eventually make it to the riverbank and into a calm eddy. This, in theory, allows you to push off any obstructions in the river with your feet, as well as keeps you from getting a foot caught on something below the water, which would likely kill you. If there's something downstream that you desperately need to avoid— say, Dead Man's Eddy—you can, in a pinch, switch over to swimming on your stomach, face-first, and kick with your feet. Although this is not overtly safe—if you were to hit an obstruction, you'd peg it square on your nose—it does get you where you want to go slightly faster, and that's a risk worth taking when the other option is likely a vicious beating and/or drowning.

According to Lakpa, Babu told him that, no matter what, they needed to both end up in the eddy on the right side of the river at the bottom of Jaws, whether they were in the kayak or out of it. He also showed Lakpa how to grab the loop attached to the front of his spray skirt and pull it off the cockpit combing, if they did happen to flip over and he couldn't roll them back over. This way, Babu explained to Lakpa, he wouldn't become trapped in the boat, upside down.

After giving his quick introduction to basic whitewater safety, Babu clambered into the back of the two-man kayak and prepared to paddle a boat that was nearly twice the length of the kayaks he was used to into a Class IV big-water maelstrom with someone who had no idea how to even swim. Krishna helped to push them free from the sandy beach and into the calm eddy in front of their camp, which was now disassembled and packed neatly away in waterproof drybags in the back of the gear raft. Shri Hari mounted a GoPro to the bow of the kayak and then got in the raft along with Madhukar, who was rowing. Resham, who was in his own solo kayak, along with Krishna, paddled alongside the raft for safety—Krishna having already been assigned as Lakpa's personal on-water savior. They paddled for almost an hour before Lakpa saw the horizon line of the river drop-off suddenly in front of him. A haze of white mist rose up from the darkness below, the jungle rising behind it. The sound was like thunder. It was Jaws.

Lakpa, Babu, and Krishna pulled off to the side of the river. They watched as the raft and Resham floated easily through the small entry waves leading into the meat of the rapid, bobbing gently up and down with the current, gradually gaining momentum. Then they watched them slam into a 6-foot-high wave and get shot clean into the air and disappear, swallowed a moment later by the crashing waves.

"I was scared," Lakpa admits.

Once in the eddy on river right at the bottom, Shri Hari climbed out of the raft, onto the riverbank, and up to the top of a small rise and turned on his video camera. He signaled with his arm for Babu and Lakpa to paddle down after them. Krishna peeled out of the eddy first, paddling down toward the immense entrance waves of Jaws alone. The idea was for him to be out of Shri Hari's shot when Babu and Lakpa came down, but to be in a position near the bottom where he could rescue them before Dead Man's Eddy, should they need it.

Babu and Lakpa paddled out of the top of the eddy. The current caught the bow, where Lakpa was sitting, and spun them around so they were facing downstream. The boat, being twice as long as the ones Babu was used to paddling, was twice as fast too, and more difficult to maneuver, at least without Lakpa knowing how to help him turn it. The entrance ripples zipped by, and they dropped into the trough of the first wave standing guard over the rest of the rapid before Babu could even get them lined up where they needed to be: farther to the left side of the river, where the raft, Resham, and Krishna had gone. They rose up with the wave and proceeded to drop into the white maw of an enormous recirculating hole. Lakpa, who went in first, closed his eyes, felt the impact of a 6-foot-tall wall of water splash on his face as the boat turned over, and pulled his skirt, as he had been instructed. A few moments later, both Babu and Lakpa were out of the boat and in the water, flushing rapidly downstream toward Dead Man's Eddy—Babu finding himself unable to roll the 12-foot tandem kayak without his partner when it was half filled with water.

Babu immediately let go of the boat and began swimming toward shore, the left shore being the closest option. He took a deep breath before his body slammed into and through each wave. Krishna paddled out of the eddy above Dead Man's on the right side of the river as fast as he could. It wasn't fast enough. He watched in horror as first Lakpa and then his brother flushed directly into the middle of the whirlpool and were sucked beneath the surface of a broiling brown-white chaos.

Without hesitation Krishna paddled in after them.

The water swirled around him, and even while sitting in a seventy-gallon boat, Krishna struggled to stay afloat and upright in the aerated water. He kept up his momentum, paddling as hard as he could into the fray, to where he saw Lakpa's head finally pop up. Before he reached him Lakpa's head disappeared again.

At the same time, Babu kicked with all his strength toward the surface. He felt himself pushed up hard against the cliff wall on river left. He found a crack in the rock with his hands and hauled himself up, so at least his head would be above the water. He took a gasping breath. His feet scratched against the wall beneath the water for a foothold. There was none.

Completely disoriented, Lakpa coughed up brown water and took hurried, frantic breaths whenever the randomness of the whirlpool brought him back up to the surface. He moved his arms and legs, aware of the futility, not knowing how to actually swim. On one of his brief stints above the water, he heard Krishna shouting for him to grab onto his kayak. Lakpa grabbed onto the metal broach loop on the bow of Krishna's boat, which allowed him to at least keep his head above the water. Krishna paddled frantically, throwing desperate high and low braces with his paddle to keep himself upright amidst the swirling current.

Babu held on to the crack in the rock wall in front of him, able to breathe but unable to do anything else. He watched as their new tandem kayak, which had followed them into Dead Man's Eddy, turned in violent circles, submerging and then reemerging, flipping end over end, sporadically.

Watching from the calm eddy above, Madhukar pulled hard on his oars, directing the raft with all of their gear directly into the whirlpool below. The experienced river guide, whom Nim Magar had sent along specifically for his skills at river rescue, figured that even though the raft was bound to get stuck it would at least have enough volume to keep them all afloat, even if they wouldn't be able to paddle it out of Dead Man's on their own. It was a quick and only partial fix. But it was the only thing he could think of at the moment to keep three of the members of his crew from drowning.

Once in Dead Man's the raft began to spin uncontrollably. It seemed content to remain upright, though, able to float above the undertows rather than fall prey to getting pulled beneath them. Madhukar let go of the oars, which weren't of much use anymore, grabbed ahold of the shoulder straps of Lakpa's PFD, and hauled him over the edge of the raft, sputtering. When the raft eventually was pushed over to the wall where Babu was, Madhukar then grabbed ahold of his shoulder straps too and pulled Babu into the boat.

Krishna, no longer hindered by the weight of Lakpa latched onto his bow, paddled as hard as he could toward the edge of the eddy, which is referred to in the paddling community (quite accurately in this case) as the eddy fence, the line where the main flow of the current meets the recirculating current of the eddy. In smaller, less powerful eddies, it forms a distinct line, capable of spinning an unsuspecting boat out of control or even flipping it. In larger, stronger eddies, like Dead Man's, the eddy fence forms a boiling wall of splashing aerated water over 10 feet wide and several feet high. This Krishna somehow managed to paddle through, upright.

Once back on shore on the opposite side of the river, Krishna hopped out of his boat. He grabbed a throw-rope, eyed the still-spinning raft, and guessed where it would be in the next three seconds. One end of the rope, tied in a loop, was clutched in his left hand. The rest was wrapped behind him, running to a small mesh-topped bag, which he picked up with his right hand. With all of his strength, he threw the bag as far as he could, halfway across the river to the raft. Madhukar caught it and attached the rope to a metal broach loop on one end of the raft. Resham and Shri Hari, who had at this point put down his camera, ran to help Krishna pull on the rope. Madhukar rowed as hard as he could. And between the three men on shore pulling on the rope and Madhukar rowing, the raft slowly inched over the eddy fence and into the downstream current.

Lakpa had managed to survive his first rapid.

Back on shore, exhausted, Babu and Lakpa watched without comment as their kayak still churned in the whirlpool. Krishna volunteered to go get it. He got back in his boat and, with one hand holding on to a carabiner tied to the end of a throw-rope, paddled upstream, back toward Dead Man's. His bow hit the eddy fence, pushed through a few feet, then stalled. Without forward momentum, Krishna's boat's stability began to waver in the frothing whitewater. After a few minutes of strenuous paddling and going nowhere, he relaxed and allowed himself to get flushed back downstream, where he rested for a few minutes before trying again. His second attempt to reenter Dead Man's was successful, but as soon as he approached the empty boat, which was still bobbing uncontrollably in the whirlpool, it dove beneath the surface and disappeared. He couldn't reach for it, for fear of flipping himself over. So Krishna kept his shoulders square and his body weight over the center of his kayak, no matter how close he came to the tandem, until he was close enough to safely clip the carabiner onto one of the boat's broach loops. He then paddled once again over the 10-foot-wide eddy fence back to the river right shoreline, where the rest of the expedition members were able to finally pull the tandem out of Dead Man's. It bobbed back toward shore heavily, like a half-sunk log.

Krishna looked at the watch he keeps on his PFD. The rescue and boat extraction had taken nearly forty-five minutes. "I was really scared. Really, really, really scared," he says.

According to Lakpa, Babu told him, "It's not really a river trip until you swallow a little water." At this, they both laughed and decided to call it a day. Tomorrow they would continue down the river.

They also realized they should probably turn on their SPOT locator again, and did so for the first time since the batteries had died nearly a week earlier back in the mountains. Suddenly, the glowing yellow dot reappeared on both the Arrufats' computer screen in Sidi and Kimberly Phinney's in San Francisco. Phinney updated the expedition blog:

04/06/2011 Ultimate Descent Team
Posted on June 4, 2011 by ruppy.kp
09:19:17 AM Begin Kayaking

———— ❧ ————

Lakpa wasn't the first person Babu had tried to teach how to paddle. Babu's wife, Susmita, was. A small woman with rich black hair and deep-brown eyes, Susmita is almost a head shorter than Babu. In 2003 she left Rampur-6 to live in Pokhara with Babu at the home of his boss, Charley Gaillard. It was the first time she had been outside their small village on the Sun Kosi. The first time she had seen roads, bicycles, cars, or buses. In 2005 she had another new experience: sitting in a kayak for the first time. They had been married for five years at that point. Their son, Niraj, was sixteen months old. Susmita was eighteen.

It's not uncommon for girls like her to be married young in Nepal. Forty-one percent of women are married, usually through a family arrangement, before they are eighteen. Ten percent, like Susmita, are married before they turn fifteen. Typically, the child brides are expected to drop out of school, move in with their older husbands, and perform domestic chores for the rest of their lives. The practice has been made illegal by modern Nepali law, but it remains unenforced—proponents of the practice citing local traditions.

Babu had wanted to share his love for kayaking with his young wife, whom he had been married to for half a decade and had had a son with, but hardly knew. He put her in one of Gaillard's old rental boats on Phewa Lake, across from the Ganesh Kayak Shop—the same exact spot he had first started kayaking. He showed her how to paddle straight, how to turn, how to brace herself with her paddle when she was about to tip over, and how to roll back upright once she had flipped over. The paddle she used was almost as thick as her tiny arms. The water was calm and cool and blue, the same as the sky.

She loved it. So much that she told Babu three years later that she wanted to become a safety kayaker and raft guide too. Just like him.

That she didn't want to just do house chores for the Gaillards and cook dal bhat anymore.

It didn't go over well.

Babu, who had been more than happy with his wife kayaking recreationally with him when she wasn't doing house chores, wondered who would take care of Niraj if they were both out guiding multiday trips. He also feared her trying to enter the male-dominated guide industry. He knew women weren't welcome there, partly because he didn't welcome them there himself. Susmita persisted, though, so he gave her an ultimatum: "It's either me or kayaking," he told her.

Susmita chose kayaking. She divorced Babu, having only recently learned that that was even an option, and took her son, Niraj, who was by then four years old, to live with Babu's parents along the banks of the Sun Kosi in Rampur-6. She returned to Pokhara to live on her own and find work as a whitewater guide. No one would hire her.

Susmita spent several months washing dishes in a local restaurant and worked on the side as a maid. Her career in whitewater looked bleak at best. She had left her husband to start a career in paddling but now hardly had any time at all to even paddle for fun, let alone have anyone pay her for it. It wasn't until Susmita met a tall, young blonde-haired, blue-eyed Swedish kayaker named Inka Trollsas that her luck changed. Trollsas had been coming to Nepal for the past decade, trying to inspire young Nepali women to kayak, and thus step out of their traditional subservient roles, through her nonprofit organization, Himalayan River Girls. Susmita fit the bill perfectly, so Trollsas invited her to come train with her and two other local female Nepali kayakers, Sita Thapa and Anu Shrestha.

The training worked. Susmita took first place in 2008 in the women's division of the Peak UK Himalayan Whitewater Challenge, where she competed with paddlers from over eleven countries for the title. Babu, who had taken second place in the men's division in both the 2004 and 2005 events but had opted out of competing that year because he had been spending more time paragliding than paddling, watched her accept a brand-new kayak during the awards ceremony.

Seeing his ex-wife win the Himalayan Whitewater Challenge prompted a change of heart in Babu. Susmita was no longer a rebellious embarrassment but a successful, talented woman. He asked her to take him back. And she did. She also went on to compete in the world freestyle championships in Switzerland and the world slalom championships in Spain, becoming the first female Nepali kayaker to compete on an international level outside of the country. She was eventually hired by Nim and Kelly Magar to work for Paddle Nepal in Pokhara.

In an interview with the *Nepali Times,* Babu later admitted in question form, "If [Susmita] had listened to me and given up kayaking, if we hadn't had a divorce, then how would my wife have become a champion?" He encouraged other Nepali women to take Susmita as an example and "follow their dreams."

Kayaking had torn Babu and Susmita apart, but it also eventually brought them together—as something more like equals. But not quite equals. Three years later, Babu told Susmita he was going to climb Everest with Lakpa, fly off of the summit, and paddle to the ocean. He wasn't asking. When Susmita told him she didn't want him to go, he went anyway, leaving her behind with Niraj and enough money to get by for a few months while he was away.

❧

Babu and Lakpa slept in late the day after they swam Jaws and Dead Man's. It was raining. After packing up camp, they got back in the kayak and paddled just over 9 miles of easy, relatively flat, fast-moving water before Lakpa saw the horizon line drop off in front of him again. A loud, distant roaring echoed in his ears. Babu told him it was a Class III+/IV- rapid named Rhino Rock, after a large horn-shaped boulder sticking up in the middle of the river near the entrance of the rapid, which they would try to veer to the right of.

Lakpa still didn't know how to turn the boat. He could only paddle forward.

"I felt a little more confident," Lakpa says, recalling the moments before dropping into Rhino Rock, which at that level was a fairly sizeable, although slightly smaller, wave train than Jaws. "It didn't feel like I was about to die. Because I knew I had two options: one is life jacket, the other is Krishna. When I flip, I realized I wouldn't die."

He was able to test his theory a few seconds later when, again, he and Babu capsized in the middle of the rapid, with Shri Hari filming the carnage from shore. Lakpa pulled his skirt and looked for Krishna, who this time was close behind him. Babu, who again was unsuccessful at rolling the tandem kayak filled with water, swam himself to shore.

"The end of the rapid is very flat water, so it was an easy rescue," Krishna says.

Easy rescue or not, Lakpa was now tired and cold after swimming two major rapids in a row. He refused to get back in the kayak with Babu.

This presented a problem for Shri Hari, who was supposed to be filming them. He couldn't make a video of them paddling a tandem kayak down the Sun Kosi if Lakpa wasn't in the boat. But Lakpa insisted on switching over to the raft, especially after learning that the next 5 miles were filled with six solid Class IV rapids—a particularly steep and challenging section of the river known as the Jungle Corridor. So Shri Hari, who had paddled a solo kayak a few times before years earlier on much easier whitewater, attached a GoPro to the bow and stern of the tandem, donned a PFD and helmet, picked up Lakpa's paddle, and climbed into the kayak along with Babu. If he couldn't film Lakpa in the kayak, he would film somebody in the kayak. And that somebody had to be him.

Krishna spent the rest of the day pulling Shri Hari and Babu out of the water. "Many, many times they went swimming," he says, having lost count of exactly how many times they capsized. They flipped on most of the six major named rapids in the Jungle Corridor.

Babu, who hadn't swam in years paddling in solo boats, couldn't quite seem to steer or even roll a tandem with an inexperienced paddler sitting in the front. But they were making headway downstream, even if it was slow and not always in the boat.

They reached the end of the Jungle Corridor at dusk and set up camp on a sandy beach. The rain had stopped. Slightly rested from his swim-free raft ride that day, Lakpa agreed to get back in the kayak and run the final rapid before the river flattened out above Chatra, their take-out, the next morning. This way Shri Hari could hopefully get at least one carnage-free shot of the both of them in the tandem before he went back to Kathmandu the next day.

The final rapid on the Sun Kosi is located just before the confluence of the Arun and Tamur, before it flattens out wide and fat and slow on the plains on the border with India. It begins with a Class III wave train and ends in a large, nearly river-wide recirculating hole called "Big Dipper." With the hole at the bottom, it's a solid Class IV. It's known for flipping and holding rafts and kayaks.

Of course, that next morning, Babu and Lakpa flipped in the hole and swam, their boat tossing itself end over end. They both flushed downstream, along with their boat. Krishna scrambled to catch up with Lakpa and pulled him to shore. "It's a very long rapid," Krishna explains. "So it was hard to catch him." By the time he did, Babu and Lakpa had lost both of their paddles.

They didn't have any spares.

IX

Mother Ganga

Koshi Tappu Wildlife Reserve, Nepal,
June 6, 2011—Approximately 290 Feet

Sitting atop ancient bicycles with old rusty chains, Babu, Lakpa, and Shri Hari rode in single file along a narrow footpath through tall grass. The sun beat down hot on their backs as the bikes squeaked beneath their weight, groaning metallically with each bump. A small cloud of dust chased them. Sporadic patches of Indian rosewood cast sun-dappled shadows on the gold-green swamps surrounding them. The Mahabharat Mountains, where they had come from just the day before, looked dark and hazy in the distance. Bristled grassbirds, swamp francolins, and Finn's weavers flew through the air. Sweat beaded on the men's foreheads and dripped slowly into their eyes. They had been biking like this all day. Headed south, vaguely toward India.

Other than knowing that they were somewhere deep within the heart of the 68-square-mile Koshi Tappu Wildlife Reserve along the Nepal/India border, and somewhere west of the Sun Kosi, none of them had any idea where they were. "We were lost," Lakpa admits. They had no maps with them. Shri Hari carried a bag with his camera gear, which he took out occasionally to film Babu and Lakpa riding in front of him through the grass. This scene grew old quickly, though, and he eventually stopped filming altogether.

Lakpa and Babu carried a few packets of dried ramen-style noodles and two water bottles, which they had purchased back in Chatra. There they had said good-bye to Madhukar and Resham, who had returned with the support raft to Kathmandu. One of Babu's friends in Chatra, Mani Kumar Rai, had lent them the bicycles when they told him they needed a way to get through the wildlife reserve.

The idea had been for Babu, Lakpa, and Shri Hari to ride the borrowed bikes through the reserve and across the India border to avoid garnering too much attention from the Indian authorities, from whom they did not have permission—namely in the form of valid visas—to enter the country. They had told the Nepali park officials on the north end of the reserve near Chatra that they intended to camp in the park. The lie worked, even though they didn't have any camping equipment. Krishna could get the kayaks and the rest of the gear across the border in a hired truck if he didn't have Shri Hari's camera gear or too many people with him, they figured. They planned to bike as fast as they could to the southern end of the reserve, meet up with Krishna and the kayaks, and then continue downstream from there.

Their water bottles were now empty. There was no sign of the river—just a flat, broad, swampy plain with a few rolling hills and trees sticking out of it as it stretched out to the horizon. Their mouths were dry when they finally saw a metal spigot on the side of the path that afternoon. They stopped, pumped the handle, and drank their fill when they saw a steady stream of off-colored water pour out of it.

Krishna, meanwhile, was parked at the India border in a hired jeep along with their two kayaks. It was the second time he had been called to negotiate on Babu and Lakpa's behalf in the past forty-eight hours. The day before, he had hired a motorboat to take him back upriver to the Big Dipper rapid, where Babu and Lakpa had swam and lost their paddles. He had discovered them in the possession of two different men on the riverside who had found each of the paddles separately. They asked Krishna for money when he requested their return. He gave the first one 200 rupees (about $2) for his trouble.

The second one he ended up giving 400 rupees (about $4) when the man said no to 200.

"Where are you going?" one of the border patrol asked him.

"Just down there," Krishna said, pointing to the beach on the river just beyond the checkpoint. The two kayaks were on top of the jeep, tied on with rope. "We're going paddling." He didn't tell the officer he was going to paddle nearly 300 miles to the ocean.

Back in the wildlife reserve, Babu, Lakpa, and Shri Hari suddenly stumbled across a paved road running perpendicular to the dirt path they were on. They turned left and headed east, figuring the river had to still be somewhere in that direction. They couldn't have passed over one of the largest rivers draining the Himalaya without noticing it. After a few minutes of easy biking on smooth pavement, they descended into a wide valley—the Sun Kosi running slow and wide through the middle of it. Eventually, they saw Krishna waiting for them with their gear at the bottom along the bank of the river.

As the sun approached the western horizon, they said good-bye to Shri Hari, who framed one last shot with his camera of Babu, Lakpa, and Krishna paddling away. Then he got into the hired jeep Krishna had taken across the border and headed back to Chatra. The next day, he caught a bus back to Kathmandu, leaving Babu, Lakpa, and Krishna to film the remainder of the expedition themselves. He didn't have a boat to use, and the raft had already returned with Madhukar and Resham to the capital, so Shri Hari couldn't follow his friends any farther. He had captured nearly one hundred hours of footage, mostly of Babu and Lakpa milling about Everest Base Camp or swimming on the Sun Kosi. The Arrufats still had the footage of the takeoff with them back in Pokhara, which Hamilton Pevec was in the midst of feverishly editing in the back room of their house.

Babu, Lakpa, and Krishna now just had to paddle about 300 miles of flat water through India, following the Sun Kosi to its confluence with the Ganges and out to the Bay of Bengal—with almost no money, and no maps to guide them.*

— ∙ —

Lakpa could now see three things in front of him: the bulbous orange bow of his and Babu's boat, murky brown water, and sky. The other side of the river was over 3 miles away, somewhere beyond a watery horizon line. The riverbank behind him was sandy and flat, like the river. They had entered the Terai in the Indian state of Bihar, the great, flat floodplains that drain the enormous snowfields of the Himalaya.

The Sun Kosi has a bad reputation in India. The river, which is nearly doubled in size after its confluence with the Arun and Tamur above Chatra, is actually referred to as the "Sorrow of Bihar." In Hindu folklore the River of Gold is said to be a woman who dreads marriage, which is a very bad thing in Hindu folklore. The monikers make sense when you consider the fact that India ranks second only to its swampy neighbor, Bangladesh, in terms of flooding casualties. The country accounts for about 20 percent of deluge-related deaths in the world, and it's primarily because of the considerable amount of water and silt the Sun Kosi carries down from Nepal into Bihar.

Almost every year during the monsoon, just south of the Nepalese border, the Sun Kosi floods to within a hair's breadth of destroying absolutely everything even remotely near it. Often, it does. In two hundred years the river's 111-mile-long outlet into the Ganges—the so-called Kosi Fan—has shifted over 120 miles from west to east. That's over half a mile per year. Outside of the Hwang Ho in China, the Sun Kosi carries more silt than any other river in the world. And

---

* It's worth noting that even if Babu, Lakpa, and Krishna had brought maps of the Ganges with them, it wouldn't have done them much good. Like the Sun Kosi Fan, the Ganges shifts its course radically through the Bihar almost every year, often cutting completely new channels miles from where it had previously flowed. Even more problematically, the government of India does not allow anyone, Indian or foreign, to buy topographic maps of any region less than 62 miles from the country's borders, which is exactly where the Ganges flows, so such useless maps don't even exist.

it dumps it all on the gridiron-flat plains of the Bihar. It's no wonder economic development has stagnated in the region. The Kosi Fan is the poorest area in India's poorest state.

The Indian government attempted to alleviate the flood problem on the Sun Kosi by building embankments along the existing river channel in the last century, hoping to contain the river. The river simply poured over the embankments and broke them, necessitating continual reconstruction at an exorbitant cost. In the years it didn't break the embankments, it backed up and flooded the land to either side, not allowing the fields to drain as they always had. Already half-drowned locals began contracting kala-azar, a horrific disease of the eyes resulting from living in perpetually waterlogged areas. The solution to the Sun Kosi's flooding problem turned out to be another problem, and a rather large one at that.

The Kosi Fan and Gangetic floodplains are so inaccessible to the police and their vehicles that poor local farmers have realized they can rob everything in sight without any real fear of being caught, let alone punished. The Bihar, the birthplace of Buddhism, has thus become known as India's lawless state. It's why Madhukar and Resham left Babu, Lakpa, and Krishna in Chatra and returned to Kathmandu with the Paddle Nepal raft. Kelly and Nim Magar, co-owners of Paddle Nepal—arguably the expedition's only real sponsor besides Peak UK and Kimberly Phinney—ordered them to return.

"I didn't want to send my raft and equipment with the Paddle Nepal company name on it in case anything should happen there," Nim says.

⤙ ⤚

After hiding their kayaks in the tall grass along the riverbank that night, Babu and Krishna went to talk to a man who was herding cattle nearby. Lakpa stayed hidden with the boats. Unlike Babu and Krishna, who had both traveled in India for kayaking, Lakpa didn't know how to speak Hindi. His two friends would have to do the talking for him so long as they were in India, even though well over three hundred different languages are actually spoken there.*

The two brothers brought back bread and some raw beef, which Krishna cooked over their small camp stove. They had no other food with them besides a few packages of dried noodles and some rice they had bought in Chatra. The plan was to pick up supplies as they went along. They set up camp that night under an orange Peak UK tarp, which had been shipped to them along with the tandem kayak by Pete Astles. They propped it up like an A-frame with two paddles, one on either side.

Before the sun rose the next morning, both Lakpa and Babu woke up feeling sick. Krishna, who hadn't imbibed the dirty well water the day before in the wildlife reserve, felt fine. The three of them quietly packed up their camp and continued downriver with Babu and Lakpa's intestines groaning. Occasionally, the two would paddle hurriedly off to the bank to relieve their illness on the sand. "Too much diarrhea," Lakpa says.

By midday they decided that it was too hot to be on the water, so they set up their tarp shelter in the grass for shade as far away from people as they could. As the sun began to set, they got on the water again, and they continued paddling until after dark, when they found a spot to camp that they deemed safe. Babu and Krishna left Lakpa to guard the hidden kayaks as they went in search of food.

"In the mountains everybody moves slowly," Lakpa says. "Everything. Even the trees are slowly growing. We come lower and lower, and people are cleverer. We don't have that much stuff. If someone took our stuff, what would we do? How would we survive?" They were all acutely aware of the danger they were in and tried their best to avoid the notoriously thievish people of the Bihar by paddling early in the day and late in the evening. Nothing attracts thieves quite like paddling a 12-foot-long bright orange boat.

---

* The Indian constitution currently recognizes twenty-two different languages as "official languages."

They set up camp each night and broke it down each morning in the dark, camouflaging their kayaks in the tall grass of the Terai, hiding in the shade of their orange tarp during the afternoon. Lakpa tried not to draw attention to himself when he was left alone with the boats, but sometimes getting noticed while standing next to two large hunks of brightly colored plastic couldn't be helped. His beard and hair had grown long and shaggy. After his recent bout of diarrhea, he looked starved. "People thought I looked like a Muslim," Lakpa says—Muslims being much more common and far less suspicious in India than a Nepali Buddhist. "Everybody that passed by would say, '*As-salamu alaykum.*'" He didn't know any Hindi to explain who he really was or what he was doing, so he didn't think it prudent to correct them. He replied with the only other phrase of Arabic he knew, "*Wa alaykumu s-salam!*" * This was usually enough to allow the Indians to affirm their assumptions and continue on their way without creating too much of a scene.

They procured an Indian cell phone, with which they called Kimberly Phinney in San Francisco almost daily. "The Ganges was big and I could provide information on which channels to take," Phinney says. "I would laugh to myself sometimes how odd it was to be sitting in the comfort of my home here in America, guiding three Nepali men down a massive river in India via Google Earth maps."

After six days in India, Lakpa began to feel immensely lethargic. The muggy heat of the lowlands, which often soaring into the nineties, made the experienced mountaineer, who claimed to smoke cigarettes up to 28,000 feet, feel ill. He was also developing a fierce waterlogged infection on one of his hands and on both of his feet. Krishna could see the white decay of infection growing on one of his own fingers and on the back of his neck. Babu's stomach still couldn't hold down food after drinking the dirty well water. He also had an infection on his neck, in the same spot as his brother. They were becoming even

---

* The Indian constitution currently recognizes twenty-two different languages as "official languages."

skinnier and more gaunt-looking than they already had been, losing weight they couldn't afford to lose. Still, each morning and night they paddled on through the brown waters of the lower Kosi, snaking their way south toward the Ganges.

Babu called Phinney one morning while standing on the side of the river just outside of Naugachia, a small, annually flood-plagued town about 5 miles from the Sun Kosi's outlet into the Ganges. Looking on her computer at the live tracking option on their SPOT locator, she told them where they were and asked how they were doing. Babu told her they were doing fine. After hanging up she updated the expedition's blog for the first time since Babu and Lakpa had started the kayaking portion of their journey a week earlier:

12/06/2011 Ultimate Descent Team
Posted on June 12, 2011 by ruppy.kp
09:24:06 AM Today the Koshi River will merge with the Ganges
River

The Ganges River is actually a goddess called Gangadevi, or Mother Ganga, at least according to Hindu mythology. It is the only river considered by a major world religion to be the physical embodiment of a deity. Created from the foot sweat of Lord Vishnu, the supreme god of Hinduism, Ganga reportedly came down from the Milky Way in response to the prayers of an ancient king named Bhagirath. His late great-grandfather, King Sagar, had apparently upset a magical hermit by the name of Kapil Muni over the matter of a stolen horse, and now a good number of his relatives were dead.

King Sagar, a prodigious procreator, had sent sixty thousand of his sixty thousand and one sons looking for the missing animal, and when they found it standing next to Muni at the southern end of

Sagar Island* in southeastern India, near present-day Bangladesh and the mouth of the Ganges, they figured that the hermit was probably the one who stole it. So they proceeded to rough him up with enthusiasm. Muni, who hadn't actually stolen the horse, incinerated King Sagar's sixty thousand sons into ashes and cursed them all to hell.

Muni then told King Sagar that the only way he could save his sons' souls was to get Gangadevi, who purified anything and everything she touched, to come down from the heavens and wash over their ashes, releasing them forever from the karmic cycle of death and rebirth—a sort of when-pigs-fly or a-cold-day-in-hell suggestion. Sagar gave his throne to his one remaining son, Amshuman, and went off into the woods to pray. He died before his prayers were answered, so Amshuman then gave the throne to his own son, Dalip, and left for the woods to pick up praying where his deceased father, Sagar, had left off. He died too.

It wasn't until Dalip's son, Bhagirath, stood on a rock on one leg high in the Himalaya near present-day Gangotri for a thousand years that Brahma, the Hindu god of creation, finally took notice and asked him what he wanted. Bhagirath told him he wanted to save the souls of his great-great-grandfather's sons. Brahma told him, sure, he'd be happy to send Ganga down to earth, but suggested that Bhagirath talk to Shiva, another Hindu god, first. Ganga couldn't come down to earth without someone to catch her fall, apparently, and Shiva would be the one to do it. Ganga would crush and drown the earth, Brahma told him. Bhagirath, unfazed, continued to balance on the rock for another ten thousand years before Shiva showed up and finally agreed to catch Ganga in the locks of his hair. Ganga didn't want to go, however, so Nandi the bull god drank her—that's why the Ganges starts at Gaumukh, the "cow's mouth." Each lock of hair formed one of the Ganges's tributaries, like the Alaknanda, Mandakini, Bhagirathi, Satluj, Indus, and Sun Kosi (just to name a few), which all feed into the Ganges from the Himalaya along its course to the sea.

---

* Sagar Island is also regularly referred to as Ganga Sagar.

Sagar's sons were finally saved, and to this day Hindus believe that anyone who bathes in Ganga's waters will be purified of all sins. And that those who have their ashes or bodies deposited in the river when they die will, likewise, be released from the perpetual karmic cycle of death and rebirth and go directly to Nirvana.

Physically, the Ganges is one of the most polluted rivers on the planet, running 1,516 miles through one of the most populated river basins in the world. Rising as an unassuming gray, silt-laden meltwater creek at about 13,000 feet from the toe of the Gangotri Glacier, just a few miles south of the Chinese border in northeastern India, Ganga's awe-inspiring beauty is tarnished quickly by the humans who worship her. Just 11 miles downstream from the source, the village of Gangotri dumps almost all of its waste directly into the river. Less than 60 miles farther south, just above the town of Uttarkashi, the Ganges is dammed up and diverted through pipes to feed turbines to generate electricity. Uttarkashi, like the rest of the cities along the Ganges, also dumps almost all of its waste into the river. Just to the south of town, a cement factory pours slurry directly into the Ganges through a pipe. Below that, the Theri Dam plugs the river up entirely, creating a reservoir over 20 miles long and 3 miles wide. The trend continues as the Ganges flows southeast toward the Bay of Bengal, where it is dammed again at Farakka by a river-wide barrage* and continually drained to precariously low levels for irrigation. Locals believe that Mother Ganga, being a purifying goddess, can't actually be polluted or destroyed.

At Varanasi, one of the holiest sites along the mighty river's banks, water samples taken from the river often contain more fecal coliform bacteria (feces) than water molecules—making the Ganges, only about halfway through its journey to the sea, a veritable river of shit. Heavy metals and toxic chemicals are dumped into it from tanneries

* A barrage is similar to a dam, but not the same. A dam stores water, creating a massive reservoir behind it, whereas a barrage is simply a weir with gates that are meant to control the flow of a river and help redirect it.

and factories built all along its banks without even a semblance of regulation. A toxic green-brown sludge forms along the water's edge, where people bathe, wash their dishes, and fetch their drinking water each day.

The Ganges is also one of the few places in the world where if you see a human body floating in the river, you don't have to call the police. Families of the recently deceased travel from all over India to deposit the remains of their loved ones in its waters, with the belief that Ganga will deliver the dead to Nirvana, the Hindu version of heaven. According to some local traditions, unmarried individuals aren't supposed to be cremated, so they are simply placed in the river, their bodies left to float downstream to decay. Many poor families can't afford to purchase enough sandalwood to properly cremate the deceased that were married, so it's not uncommon to see a partially burnt body washed up on shore or swirling idly in a trash-filled eddy. Feral dogs prowl the river edge, feeding on the corpses.

In eastern Bihar, where the Ganges joins with the Sun Kosi, the river is sluggish, moving no more than 2 miles per hour through a broad, flat plain stretching off as far as the eye can see. The water and surrounding air are warm and sticky—a far cry from the raging glacial torrents of either the Ganga's or Sun Kosi's Himalayan headwaters. There are few towns or even villages. As the river approaches the coast, it begins to divide and subdivide into a labyrinth of smaller rivers, eventually seeping obscurely into the ocean through a vast mangrove forest inhabited by man-eating tigers and poisonous snakes.

It is a long, hard road to Nirvana.

◆━━◆

Although it had been raining for the past several days, a full moon covered Babu, Lakpa, and Krishna's camp in a silver half-light. The tepid water at the edge of the riverbank glinted brightly with it. It was the team's fourth night on the Ganges, and they could see clear across the river to the tall grass on the other side, even though it was a little before 11:00 p.m. and, otherwise, completely dark. The night before, they had woken up in the midst of a light rain next to a corpse. "A dog was eating it," Lakpa says. The lower half of the body was missing.

On this full-moon night, their tarp shelter lay collapsed on the ground at their feet, covered in sand. One of the corner stakes had been pulled out. Lakpa counted nine shadowy faces standing around them. None of them looked pleased. He couldn't understand what Babu and Krishna were saying to them, or what they said in return, but he knew it wasn't good.

Suddenly, one of the shadowy strangers grabbed Lakpa's wallet out of his pocket. Lakpa shoved him hard in the chest, knocking the man over. Krishna began to shout in Hindi. Babu held up his own wallet, offering it to the men, who were obviously now even more angry than they had been before. They took it, along with Lakpa's wallet and mobile phone, and moved off grumbling into the grass. In a matter of a few minutes, the Nepalis had lost all of their money and their only means of communication with the outside world besides their GPS tracker, which was stashed in one of the boats.

They hurriedly packed up camp, shoving their collapsed tarp shelter unceremoniously into the back of the tandem kayak. The moon continued to shine, as if nothing had happened. Getting into their boats, they could hear the strange men returning. They could hear voices getting closer through the tall grass. They had nothing more to give them besides their boats and their lives, and they didn't care to wait around to find out which they would take next.

They then paddled out to the center of the river and pointed their bows downstream, watching as the thieves collected on the shoreline where their camp had been, shouting after them. After a few minutes they heard a motor start. Looking behind them, they could see a small wooden fishing boat pursuing them slowly across the surface of the smooth, silver-colored water. After a few minutes of frantic paddling, they realized that the boat wasn't gaining on them. It evidently had a small motor.

The next few hours proved to be a surreal, slow-speed on-water chase: a handmade rowboat with a tiny outboard motor, filled with bandits, chasing three Nepali kayakers in the moonlight along the Ganges through the Indian Terai. Babu, Lakpa, and Krishna remained silent as they paddled as fast as they could, which seemed to keep them about 100 yards ahead of the boat. It was a losing battle, they knew. Unless their pursuers ran out of gas soon, the kayakers couldn't keep up the pace long enough to stay ahead of them all night.

Then the moon began to go dark. The silver-shrouded plains faded into black. The water around them lost its inky sheen. They paid little attention to the slight change in light, but it was there, growing darker by the minute. By 11:53 p.m. the sky was completely black. That's when they noticed there was a gaping hole in the sky where the moon had been just a few minutes before. It was a full lunar eclipse—a complete blackout. The last one had been forty years earlier, on August 6, 1971. The next isn't expected until June 15, 2058.[*]

Babu, Lakpa, and Krishna paddled toward a grassy island in the middle of the river. Once on shore, they quickly tucked themselves and the boats into the weeds, hoping the newfound darkness would help them avoid detection. Then they waited, listening to the sound of the motorboat move down the river past them. When the eclipse ended and moonlight flooded the plains once more, they could still see the boat puttering downstream in the distance. They could do nothing as they watched it turn around and putter upstream straight back at them.

"They went up and down the river, looking for us all night and most of the morning," Lakpa says. With daylight, the men in the boat

---

[*] A full lunar eclipse, as opposed to a partial lunar eclipse, occurs when the centers of the moon, earth, and sun are in near-perfect alignment. It's a rare occasion, but when it does happen, the atmosphere also plays a role in how dark a lunar eclipse will be. If the sky is clear, it may allow some refracted light to stray onto the moon's surface, making the eclipse not quite as dark as it otherwise would be. On the night of June 15, 2011, when Babu, Lakpa, and Krishna were being chased by bandits down the Ganges, the sky was made even darker with the help of the ash thrown into the atmosphere by the recent eruption of Iceland's most active volcano, Grímsvötn, as well as the ash still present in the atmosphere from the 2010 eruption of Eyjafjallajökull.

left, motoring downstream where Babu, Lakpa, and Krishna knew they had to follow.

After a few minutes of nerve-wracking paddling, wondering if the boatmen were hiding in the weeds and waiting for them, Babu, Lakpa, and Krishna came around a left-facing bend in the river. The river itself is miles wide, interspersed with flat sandbars leading down stagnant dead-end channels. In the distance they could see a low, faint line running across the water through the morning haze: the Farakka Barrage. They could also see that the boat that had been chasing them was now on river left, which they didn't know at the time leads into Bangladesh. They paddled to river right, where some men with guns promptly stopped them.

— —

The Farakka Barrage is more than 1.5 miles long, stretching the entire width of the Ganges at its most narrow point as it turns east into Bangladesh. It forces a significant portion of the river's water into a 23-mile-long concrete-lined feeder canal that leads to the Hugli River, which then flows out through Kolkata to the Bay of Bengal. The barrage consists of 108 iron gates that either allow some of the river to flow along its natural course into neighboring Bangladesh or don't. More often than not, they don't. Bangladesh isn't happy about it, but there's not much they can do. The barrage is on Indian soil and protected twenty-four hours a day, seven days a week, by armed guards posted every 65 feet along its length. Photography is strictly prohibited. It's also very likely the largest man-made structure in the world that doesn't actually work. At least, not the way it was supposed to.

The problem with Farakka begins nearly 220 miles south at the port city of Kolkata on the banks of the Hugli River. As far back as 1852, the East India Company was worried about the long-term viability of the port, which they controlled at the time. It was silting up, getting shallower every year. It was a natural thing. The mouth of the

Hugli had been continually silting up and changing its course to the sea for thousands of years. The East India Company predicted, correctly, that this would eventually pose a fairly serious problem to the shipping industry there.

A British engineer named Sir Arthur Cotton was the first to suggest that the mighty Ganges River, running hundreds of miles to the north into Bangladesh, could actually be diverted down into the Hugli and thus (theoretically) clear out the silt from the port of Kolkata with the extra flow it would generate through the port. The idea was considered briefly, then rejected. In 1930, as the Hugli continued to get shallower, the Bengal Chamber of Commerce reconsidered the idea but again rejected it. Later the Indian government took the idea seriously enough to study it for twenty years: from 1951 to 1971. Then, without any international agreement with Bangladesh, from which they would be diverting the water and which was at that time still part of Pakistan, they built the barrage. It took five years. A small town cropped up beside the barrage in the middle of the Terai to house the workers who were constructing it. The town, called Farakka Barrage Township, was laid out as a grid, neatly subdivided by letter and number into row after row of anonymous cream-colored concrete buildings surrounded by barbed wire.

Unfortunately, Farakka Barrage didn't work. The port of Kolkata is still getting shallower. Nothing has changed, except that Bangladesh is now receiving half the water from the Ganges it once did and flooding in the Bihar has gotten even worse. The waters of the Ganges just flood around Farakka's embankments, which, similar to the ones on the Sun Kosi, need to be regularly rebuilt. Now that less of the Ganges flow is going into Bangladesh along its original course, salt water from the Bay of Bengal has also crept almost 60 miles farther up into the Sunderbans than it had previously been able to, in effect killing a large portion of the world's largest mangrove forest.* There's also a

---

* It's also quite likely that Bangladesh's growing population has something to do with the decline in the Sunderbans mangrove forests, but the lower water level of the Ganges certainly doesn't help the situation.

significant amount of silt building up behind the barrage itself, which continually needs to be dredged to allow what little boat traffic there is through the gates.

—

Talking to the guards, Babu told the armed men standing on the shore that he and his companions were actually Indians traveling back to Kolkata from Darjeeling. It was an exceedingly unlikely story. Darjeeling is over 200 miles to the north of Farakka.

"Why didn't you just take a bus or the train?" they asked, eyeing the two odd-looking, bright orange and red boats.

"Too expensive," Babu said. "How much is it to get through the gate?"

They told him 22,000 Indian rupees (about $360). Babu, Lakpa, and Krishna had no money among the three of them after being robbed the night before. They didn't even have that much to begin with when they started out from Lukla. Babu told the guards about the robbery. This got them an invitation to the nearby guardhouse to have some food, for which Babu, Lakpa, and Krishna were very grateful. They hadn't eaten in over twenty-four hours. The guards told Babu and Krishna—Lakpa couldn't understand what they were saying in Hindi—that they couldn't let them through the barrage without payment, but they could let them walk around it with their boats to the feeder canal, which leads to the Hugli River. "That's the way you want to go, if you're trying to get to Kolkata," the guards told them. "The other gate leads to Bangladesh."

After thanking the guards for their help, Babu, Lakpa, and Krishna retrieved their boats and carried them up and over the embankment to the concrete-lined feeder canal on the other side. They paddled across and set up their camp on the left side of the canal, opposite of Farakka Barrage Township. Leaving Lakpa once again with the gear, Babu and Krishna paddled the tandem across to the town, found a phone, and put in a call to Phinney in San Francisco.

"They had been robbed of all their money," Phinney says. "They had a tough time getting around the dam and were tired and unsure what to do. They had no water left and food was again running low." She told them that she would wire them some money via Western Union, which she knew after a quick Google search had a branch in Farakka. After collecting the money from the bank, Babu and Krishna purchased more food and water and brought it back across the river to Lakpa. The next morning they continued paddling south through the feeder canal toward Kolkata, still over 180 miles away.

Phinney updated the blog:

17/06/2011 Ultimate Descent Team
Posted on June 17, 2011 by ruppy.kp
05:53:52 AM After a few days of trouble near Farakka, we have left the main stream of the ganges, and are continuing through India via the Hooghly River . . . Manys days of rain and little food..

Two days later, she updated it again:

19/06/2011 Ultimate Descent Team
Posted on June 19, 2011 by ruppy.kp
08:45:22 AM Still kayaking, see Gps for location

During that time, Babu, Lakpa, and Krishna paddled steadily on, covering nearly 20 miles per day. They could see the white, pus-filled infections growing steadily on their feet, hands, and bodies. They stayed in ashrams, temples built to help house religious pilgrims along the banks of the Ganges, whenever they could. During the nights they couldn't find an ashram, they picked a forsaken spot on the shoreline and pitched their tarp. Babu and Krishna explained away the oddity of themselves and their boats being there by telling anyone who asked that they were pilgrims on their way to Ganga Sagar, the official holy end of the Ganges. This was partly true, although slightly misleading in the fact that they weren't religious pilgrims. They were adventuring pilgrims.

"A few people asked us where we had bought the boats," Lakpa says. They were interested in buying either one of the ones that Babu and Lakpa or Krishna was paddling, or a new one of their own. "We told them we got the boats in Kolkata," Lakpa says. Babu or Krishna would then give them a fake number to a factory that didn't exist.

Nine days after leaving Farakka, the team paddled into Kolkata, a bustling metropolis of over fourteen million people. The skyscrapers were the closest things to mountains they had seen in weeks. They had been on the river for twenty-one days and looked remarkably out of place floating through the city in their bright red and orange plastic boats. So out of place, some policemen standing on the shoreline called out for them to stop.

"We just waved and said, '*Namaste!*'" Lakpa recalls. They just kept paddling. The police officers, lacking a boat, could do little more than watch them go.

A few miles downstream, they stopped under a bridge next to a pile of garbage. They buried the kayaks and their gear under the garbage, walked into town, and ordered a large pizza.

Babu, Lakpa, and Krishna knew they were getting close to the ocean. They could see the river rise and lower each day with the tide. Babu and Krishna, who had never seen the ocean before, thought this odd. They hadn't heard of tides. Phinney told them that night over the phone that the southern tip of Sagar Island was only about 50 miles to the south. They were sick, tired, and covered in sores but almost done with the first-ever Everest summit-to-sea expedition.

Ironically, the only other person to have completed a similar feat did it in reverse, twenty-one years earlier.

On February 5, 1990, a lanky, dark-haired Australian named Tim Macartney-Snape went for a swim in the Bay of Bengal on the southern tip of Sagar Island—the very same beach on which Babu and

Lakpa were about to end their expedition—and then walked through northeastern India to Nepal, where he then climbed Mount Everest via the South Col route, solo. It took him just over three months, almost the same amount of time it took Babu and Lakpa to climb Everest and descend to the ocean. It was more or less the same trip Babu and Lakpa were about to finish, just backward, without paragliding or kayaking.

Macartney-Snape also had an entourage of support drivers, film crew, sherpas, liaison officers, and his wife, although he insisted on carrying all of his own supplies in an effort to maintain some semblance of self-sufficiency. Notably, he climbed Everest without the aid of supplemental oxygen. Afterward he claimed that he was the first person to have truly climbed all of Everest's 29,035 feet, which technically was correct. No one else had ever traveled from sea level to the top of Everest without the aid of some sort of motorized vehicle. Macartney-Snape also made a movie and wrote a book about his expedition, each one titled *Everest: From Sea to Summit,* and then started his own gear company, which he called, not surprisingly, Sea to Summit.

A man wearing a loincloth stood barefoot at the edge of Ganga Sagar. He was alone on the beach. A dense, dark green jungle reared up out of the sand about a half mile behind him. The ocean was gray, reflecting the clouds above. It was difficult to tell, looking out at the horizon, where the water stopped and the sky began. He turned and watched, with no visible display of surprise, as three men paddled slowly past him out of the mangrove forest in two brightly colored little boats and into the shore break—as if they were going to just keep paddling straight out into the Bay of Bengal. He had no idea they'd come all the way from the summit of Mount Everest: over 500 miles from the top of the world.

Water splashed over the bows of Babu, Lakpa, and Krishna's boats as they paddled through the 3-foot-high waves hitting the shore. The spray of the ocean tasted salty on their lips. There was no more river ahead of them, just a broad, flat, gray horizon line. Their summit-to-sea journey was over, but Lakpa was too tired to sing.

The final 50-mile push to the ocean had passed without much fanfare or incident, other than Babu, Lakpa, and Krishna getting into a fistfight with a group of Bangladeshis over their choice of a campsite their second night out of Kolkata. It had turned out to be on a brick factory's private property. The factory workers weren't pleased. After a few swings were taken, the police were called, broke up the fight, and then sent Babu, Lakpa, and Krishna on their way. It had taken three days for them to travel from Kolkata to the southern tip of Sagar Island, to end their journey on an empty beach. A lone man in a loin-cloth was the only other witness to the successful completion of the first-ever Everest summit-to-sea expedition.

Back on the beach, they asked the man in the loincloth to take their picture. He clicked the shutter once, handed back the camera, and then wandered off. Babu unpacked the mobile and called Phinney in the United States. He told her they had made it to the ocean, but that they were going to leave now, because there were "strange scorpi-ons" on the beach. He would learn later that the scorpions he had seen were actually just harmless crabs. Regardless, they were all ready to be done. It was just after 1:00 p.m., just under three months after they had set out from Kathmandu for Everest.

After a brief conversation with Phinney, Krishna snapped a few more still photos of Babu and Lakpa sitting on the tandem kayak next to the ocean. Before they left, he took a short video of them dunk-ing themselves into the ocean. Then the three of them got back into their kayaks and paddled inland, retracing half of the distance they had already paddled that day, 10 miles back to the town of Kakdwip, where they got a hotel, had a few beers to celebrate the end of their journey, and fell asleep.

They had spent only about thirty minutes on the beach that marked the end of their journey, about half the time they had spent on the summit of Mount Everest. It was the end of what they had dubbed "the ultimate descent": the first complete, continuous, nonmotorized descent of Mount Everest.

Phinney updated the blog:

27/06/2011 Ultimate Descent Team
Posted on June 27, 2011 by ruppy.kp
01:23:06 PM BAY OF BENGAL, EXPEDITION FINISH
big waves and the water is very salty, so happy to be finish!!!!!

Epilogue

Sarangkot, Nepal,
February 10, 2012—Approximately 2,925 Feet

Babu and Lakpa sit side by side on a low berm covered in dry, brown grass. Rising up behind them, the Annapurna Massif stands out starkly from a clear blue sky like an enormous white shark fin. Little yellow flowers cover the hillside around them, scattering the otherwise brown landscape with random bursts of color. The bright red, green, and yellow crescents of paragliders circle overhead, rising and falling through the air over the darker blue of Phewa Lake, over 1,000 feet below. The city of Pokhara forms a haphazard grid along the eastern shore.

Lakpa and Babu are both wearing neon green and black long-sleeved shirts emblazoned with the paragliding company Niviuk's logo—the same company that made the wing they used to fly off Everest almost eight months earlier. The company does not officially sponsor them. Niviuk just sent them each a free shirt. Each is also wearing a new khaki-colored Sup'Air baseball cap—sent by the company that manufactured the harnesses they used to fly off Everest, and that Lakpa used for climbing it. Similarly, the company doesn't officially sponsor Babu and Lakpa. They had just sent them free gear to use on the expedition, and now the hats.[*]

---

[*] At the time of the interview being described, neither Niviuk nor Sup'Air officially sponsored Babu or Lakpa. The same held true as this book was published. However, both companies did sponsor Babu at the 2013 Red Bull X-Alps event, Niviuk by giving him a brand-new wing and Sup'Air by providing him with a new lightweight harness and backpack. Sup'Air also provided for free the harnesses that Babu and Lakpa used on Everest.

Four people stand in front of them: Kimberly Phinney; David Arrufat's girlfriend, Mukti; a Kathmandu-based British ultramarathon runner/reporter named Richard Bull; and Alex Treadway, a London-based cameraman for *National Geographic Adventure*. The air is cool. Everyone is wearing jackets, except Babu and Lakpa, who sit slightly hunched in the grass, cradling themselves against the light winter winds of the Himalayan foothills in order to show off their new shirts during their film interview.

Treadway, a tall thirty-seven-year-old with a buzzed head and kind brown eyes, stands slightly off to the side, about 10 feet in front of Babu and Lakpa, in a black hooded sweatshirt. Immediately to his right is a video camera attached to the top of a black tripod. He has flown with it from London and taken the nine-hour bus ride to Pokhara from Kathmandu in order to film the two men in front of him for the magazine. Mukti, dressed in a light blue jacket and wool stocking cap, sits immediately in front of Babu and Lakpa, holding a large microphone. It's covered with a wind muffler that makes it look a bit like a small gray dog. She holds it up to their faces, just out of the camera shot. Bull and Phinney stand just to the right of Treadway, arms crossed, looking at Lakpa and Babu. Phinney has just flown a red-eye over 7,000 miles from her home in San Francisco, at her own expense. It's the second time she has come to Nepal since Babu and Lakpa completed their Everest expedition—the first time, she was the only one interviewing them. Bull, a friend of Treadway who was asked to help with the interview, is holding a sheet of paper with a series of questions written on it that he has been asking Babu and Lakpa to answer for the camera for the past twenty minutes. Phinney has been coaching them on what to say, occasionally asking questions in addition to the written ones.

"And so my dear Babu and Lakpa," Phinney says, "how does it feel to be National Geographic Adventurer of the Year 2012?" There is a moment of silence. Babu and Lakpa look at her, obviously puzzled.

"Both of us, honestly, we don't know," Babu tells her, making sure to keep the smile on his face. "We are always far from other media, and this is new. . . . We don't know what's happening. We don't know what *National Geographic* is. We are still confused, what this is. We want to know."

Babu and Lakpa had just won possibly the most prestigious prize for outdoor adventure athletes in the world. Each year since 2005, the Adventure branch of the US-based National Geographic Society has nominated ten of the world's best outdoor adventure athletes to compete for the title of Adventurer of the Year. It is ultimately chosen by popular vote on *National Geographic*'s website, which receives over nineteen million unique views per month. That year, over 72,000 votes had been cast, and Babu and Lakpa had won in a landslide, despite garnering hardly any media attention after actually completing their expedition. They beat out professional Western athletes with highly organized and highly marketed social media campaigns, without even trying. Or even knowing what the award was that they were supposedly "competing" for.

The other nominees included the American climber Corey Richards, who had summited Pakistan's 26,358-foot Gasherbrum II, the thirteenth-highest mountain in the world, without supplemental oxygen or the help of porters, in winter; an Austrian woman named Gerlinde Kaltenbrunner, who was the first woman to summit all fourteen of the world's 8,000-meter peaks without supplemental oxygen or the help of porters; and an American named Jennifer Pharr Davis, who hiked all 2,181 miles of the Appalachian Trail in forty-six days, eleven hours, and twenty minutes, averaging 47 miles a day. Just to name a few.

Babu's friend Erik Boomer, the twenty-seven-year-old American kayaker and photographer who had taken him off his first 40-foot waterfall when he was nineteen, was also nominated that year along with his expedition partner, then sixty-five-year-old Arctic adventurer and writer Jon Turk. They had become the first people to circumnavigate Canada's Ellesmere Island, a 104-day 1,485-mile route, which they did mainly by pulling their gear-laden boats over ice on skis. A polar bear ripped through the side of their tent, and they nearly ran out of food. When they finished Turk was immediately hospitalized. His kidneys, along with a good number of his bodily functions, had just stopped working. "Doctors tell me that in that wonderland of sea and ice, my body was on the brink of collapse," Turk would later write in an article for *Canoe & Kayak*. "And [my] brain said, 'Not yet, old friend. We're in this together, you and me, brain and urinary tract. Hang on. You can shut down after we get to town.'"

"Being nominated for that award was one of the greatest honors I've received," Boomer says. He hadn't even heard of his friend's Everest expedition until he saw Babu's name mentioned in the list of fellow nominees. "I was like, 'Holy shit.' I couldn't think of a better person to win it. As much as I wanted to have the award, I definitely didn't want anybody else to have it but Babu." So Boomer went online and cast his own vote for Babu and Lakpa.[*]

Previous nominees for the award had included such notable outdoor adventurers as Alex Honnold, who in 2010 climbed both the iconic 2,000-foot Regular Northwest Face of Half Dome and the 2,900-foot Nose route up El Capitan in California's Yosemite Valley, solo, in under twenty-four hours;[†] Dean Potter, who in 2008 BASE jumped off Switzerland's 13,025-foot Eiger in a wingsuit, setting the record for the world's longest BASE jump ever; and Colin Angus and Julie Wafaei, who spent nearly two years walking, cycling, skiing, and rowing around the world, covering nearly 26,000 miles.

In simplified English, Bull says, "Many people voted. You know? Because you were on one website with ten other people, all these big mountain climbers, these famous people doing other big journeys, but many people, they chose you, they selected you. They thought you were the number one adventurers in the whole world—the WHOLE

---

[*] It's worth noting that voters for the National Geographic Adventurer of the Year Award are allowed to vote multiple times, but only once daily. Boomer actually voted for Babu every day for the duration of the voting period, instead of for himself and Turk.

[†] A week later, the twenty-five-year-old Honnold and his climbing partner, Shawn Leary, also managed to climb the Nose on El Capitan three times in one day, breaking the speed record for consecutive ascents on the route.

world. They thought you were the best ones. You were the best adventurers in the world in 2012. What do you think of what people think?"

Babu and Lakpa don't quite know what to make of it. They are still a bit confused as to where this supposed big award actually is. No one has told them that they aren't being given anything tangible. No cash prize. No trophy.* No certificate. Just a title. And that means absolutely nothing to them. They have just been awarded one of the highest honors an adventure athlete can receive, and they don't care.

Treadway interjects patiently with a light British accent, "I mean, you're very popular. Everybody is very inspired by what you've achieved by your ultimate descent. So everybody has chosen you as their favorite adventurers of the year. How do you feel?"

"Just a minute," Babu says. "I'm confused. I'm not really clear. I'm confused." Lakpa stays silent, looking at the ground.

"Well, Babu," Phinney says, "*National Geographic* isn't going to tell the world until February 28. So you need to keep the secret as best you can. Only for you. Not for David. Not for Blue Sky Paragliding. Nobody can know this. You're first place, out of everybody who got looked at in the world. You guys are number one to the world!"

"Wooo! Now I understand," Babu says, not really understanding. "Before, because questions coming, and I still confused. What is question?"

"Let's try this again," Phinney says. "So Babu and Lakpa, the world has chosen you as Adventurers of the Year. What would you like to say to the world?"

Lakpa suddenly chimes in. "Thank you very much, all over people." He says it slowly, enunciating every syllable. His English isn't as good as Babu's, he thinks, so he has chosen to speak as little as possible during the interview.

"And thank you to the people who give the opportunity to us to share our dream all over the world," Babu says. "Our thanks to our

---

* Up until 2012 *National Geographic* gave the winners of the award a small plaque. It discontinued the plaques the year Babu and Lakpa won the award.

Hanuman Airlines team, Kimberly and David, and most thank you for *National Geographic*, sharing our experience and our dream all over the world. And thank you to everyone who supported us. All of our friends who supported us in the kayaking part and the climbing part and the Nepalis outside of the country. Now maybe we did something interesting for people all over the world."

As she has done throughout the interview, Phinney asks the same question again. She told them at the beginning that if she did this, they needed to shorten their answer.

"Uh, thank you very much for all the people, and all the friends, and everyone who supported us," Babu says hastily. "Thank you. Thank you very much. We don't have anything more to say. We say thank you very much. I don't know . . ." He and Lakpa bow slightly toward the camera as he says it, hands pressed together in front of them.

"Just as the tape is running out," Treadway says, glad to have an ending he can actually use. He has been recording for fifty-eight minutes. The final video of the interview eventually will be cut down to two minutes, twenty-six seconds. "That's fantastic," he says, and cuts the camera.

❧

On July 2, 2011, Phinney once again updated the expedition blog:

> *02/07/2011 The Ultimate Descent Team*
> *Posted on July 2, 2011 by ruppy.kp*
> *Finish Challenge, back home with our family's, after a week travel to get back into Nepal*

It had been four days since Babu, Lakpa, and Krishna had actually finished their expedition. Leaving the town of Kakdwip, they had strapped their two kayaks to the top of a hired jeep* with some rope and

---

* In Nepal and India, the term *jeep* is commonly used to refer to any sport utility vehicle. Babu, Lakpa, and Krishna likely hired a TATA brand jeep, although none of them remember for certain.

driven back to the India/Nepal border. It took two days. It had taken them three weeks to paddle the same distance. Phinney needed to wire them additional money through Western Union in Kakdwip to pay for it.

At the border they found David Arrufat waiting for them. He had driven the Blue Sky Paragliding van all day down from Pokhara to pick them up. They couldn't bring an Indian vehicle into Nepal, so they needed a ride from someone with Nepali plates.

"He brought beer," Lakpa says. They got drunk and sang all the way to Chitwan, about a four-hour drive from Kathmandu, where they stopped and spent the night. The next day, Lakpa was reunited with his wife, Yanjee, and his four-year-old son, Mingma Tashi, at their home. He had been gone three months, but he had kept his promise to come back alive, for which Yanjee was grateful. Arrufat, Babu, and Krishna had to wait an additional two days before they could make it back to their homes in Pokhara, where Babu was once again reunited with his wife, Susmita, and his son, Niraj. A landslide had taken out a large section of the Prithvi Highway, blocking the only road in or out of the city from the east.

Lakpa and Babu's friends and families welcomed them home as heroes, but not many people inside or outside of Nepal actually knew what they had just accomplished. Aside from the short blogs posted by Arrufat on APPIfly.org and the one *Cross Country* magazine posted on its website, XCmag.com, the day after Babu and Lakpa had flown from Everest, there had been very little coverage of their expedition in the media at that point.* There had been absolutely none whatsoever

---

* In the week after they flew from the summit, Babu and Lakpa's flight from Everest was also briefly mentioned in blog posts on Outsideonline.com, Gadling.com, and GrindTV.com, which repurposed content from the original XCmag.com story and listed Lakpa and Babu's exploits on the mountain along with other noteworthy happenings on Everest that week. Also featured were Alpine Ascents International expedition members Garrett Madison, Tom Halliday, and Michael Horst, who became the first climbers to stand atop two 8,000-meter peaks within a twenty-four-hour period (summiting Everest and neighboring Lhotse the same day); Bhakta Kumar Rai (aka "Supreme Master God Angel"), who had stayed on top of Everest for thirty-two hours straight just before Babu and Lakpa had flown from the summit; and RMI Expeditions guide Dave Hahn, who summited Everest for the thirteenth time that same week.

in Nepal. And it wasn't for lack of trying, at least on Phinney and the Arrufats' part.

"We worked twenty-four hours a day to share information [about the expedition]," David Arrufat says. "And nobody took it. *National Geographic* . . . all the magazines. We wrote perhaps one thousand e-mails to everybody, all the listing of media in the world. We wrote to the newspaper, we sent the information. Nobody took it."

Phinney, likewise, was ferociously sending e-mails to media outlets in multiple countries, but received little response at first. She had even gone so far as to fly over to Nepal immediately after the expedition to record an interview with Babu and Lakpa in Pokhara, which she then used to provide quotes to the few magazines she did eventually hear back from. The only success they had initially in spreading the story came in the form of a 266-word article on *Australian Geographic*'s website, which wasn't posted until August 22.

Along with the apparent lack of interest in their accomplishment, Lakpa suddenly found himself with a bill for $15,000. It was from Himalayan Trailblazer, the guide company that had outfitted the Everest portion of their expedition. The company apparently no longer thought officially sponsoring Lakpa and Babu's expedition was in its best interest.* And it wanted its investment back.† However, the company created and continued to maintain a Facebook profile for "the Ultimate Descent," as well as another website for the expedition: theultimatedescent.wordpress. com. In response, Phinney updated the homepage of her own website for the expedition, theultimatedescent.com, stating, in all red:

*(****ATTENSION PLEASE BE ADVISED WE DO NOT HAVE A FACEBOOK PAGE, WE R NOT AFFILATED OR IN COMMUNICATION WITH THE OWNER OF THAT PAGE OR THE WEB SITE ATTACHED TO IT****)*

---

* Himalayan Trailblazer refused to comment for this book.

† As of December 2012, Lakpa was still paying Himalayan Trailblazer back.

Part of the reason they were having such trouble selling the story was likely because they were expecting a lot of money for it. "Nobody wanted to pay for photos," David says. Phinney claims that he was asking thousands of dollars for exclusive photo rights to the expedition. "I don't remember how much I was asking," Arrufat says. What they didn't know is that magazines have a set, standard photo rate for the images they run, and that they rarely have any budget to negotiate on those terms. And rarely do they want exclusive photo rights, unless they're planning to run them as a cover image or a feature in the print edition of the publication.

Phinney sent her own e-mail to *National Geographic Adventure* on August 16:

> *We have just submitted our press release and were hoping you might be interested in publishing our expedition story as well. At the current moment we have not done a full Exclusive nor have we released most of photos to any publications yet. We have a select 4 that we are giving away for free. All others still have not been released. We have over 4000 of some of the most amazing photos i have ever seen. The flying ones are incredible and show the curvature of the earth. We would love to have a full Exclusive in National Geographic, if this story is of interest to you please contact me as soon as possible. Again we have yet to give an exclusive and I feel very strongly that National Geographic would be the best representative of our story and photos.*
>
> *Please contact us if you are interested*
> *Kimberly Phinney*

She followed up again on August 23:

> *Just checking in again. I am still with holding photos and full details of this expedition as i fully believe the story and photos are worth getting in a good publication. I never heard back from you*

weather you were interested in this story or not. I have been fol-
lowing you publication for a while now and it seems perfect for
your magazine, the photos themselves are incredible, many from the
flight showing the full curvature of the earth. I do want to tell you
the details of the story are just as amazing, as the whole expedition
was amazing. If you could please respond and notify me if you have
intrest I would greatly appreciate it. I wil not settle untill I get the
coverage of this story that it deserves. I also want to advise you we
are in final stages of editing a 30min documentary of the hike and
flight part of this journey. The guys were able to film some amazing
shots of this expedition as well, including the take off and flight. I
am 100% confident in saying that no one else has this kind of foot-
age of Everest and surrounding region.
  Cheers,
  Kimberly Phinney

Mary Anne Potts, the editor of *National Geographic Adventure,*
wrote back a few hours later. She said that the magazine was considering doing a story that would possibly run in November. "It's not
necessary for us to have the exclusive," Potts added. "You can share it
with other media."

Meanwhile, Hamilton Pevec, the Coloradan who had been editing
the GoPro footage from Babu and Lakpa's flight from Everest, as well
as the interview footage Mukti took shortly after they had landed, had
finished a rough cut of the film back in Pokhara. Consulting with the
Arrufats, who were the producers, he titled the twenty-eight-minute
documentary *Hanuman Airlines,* a nod to the flying Hindu monkey
god adorning the storefront of the Blue Sky Paragliding shop. Baloo's
brother, Pradeep Basel, and his friend Kiran Punja wrote and recorded
the music for the film in a single afternoon at a small recording studio
in Pokhara.

"It was a glorified slideshow," Pevec says. "My biggest regret is not
being able to tell the whole thing. There were so many amazing details

that got left out of the film. Of course the most obvious: the whole kayak portion of the journey." In the film Babu and Lakpa's entire thirty-seven-day journey from where they landed their paraglider in Namche Bazaar to the ocean is covered in less than sixty seconds. There's no video. Just still photos, which Babu gave David to use in the film.

It appeared as if the bulk of the expedition was merely an afterthought.

Still, the film was accepted to the Coupe Icare Free Flight International Film Festival in Saint-Hilaire, France, that year, which had been the Arrufats' main goal for the project to begin with. According to Pevec, "Using it as a promotional device was part of the big plan to launch APPI," the Arrufats' new paragliding instructor certification organization. David procured visas and tickets for both Babu and Lakpa to join him in France September 22–25, so they could attend the premiere of the movie that covered at least the paragliding portion of their expedition.

Shri Hari, the expedition's cameraman, was annoyed that Babu had gone behind his back to edit another film about their trip without him. After refusing to share his kayak footage with Pevec for use in *Hanuman Airlines,* he and Lakpa proceeded to start making their own feature-length film about the expedition. They decided to focus it almost exclusively on Lakpa, "since *Hanuman Airlines* is Babu's story," Shri Hari says, and titled it *The Flying Sherpa.* It would take them over two years to complete it, and likewise, the paddling portion of the video lasts only a few minutes. The film is still only available in Nepal. Babu had nothing to do with its production. "It is Lakpa's film," Babu says.

At the same time, Phinney provided the transcript of her initial interview with Babu and Lakpa about the expedition to both *Cross Country* and *Canoe & Kayak* to use in articles for their respective upcoming November/December issues—which would appear in print nearly five months after the expedition had actually finished.* They

---

* The author of this book, Dave Costello, wrote the article about Babu and Lakpa's expedition for *Canoe & Kayak.* It was titled "The Ultimate Source to Sea."

would prove to be the only two media outlets that would actually pay Babu and Lakpa for their photos.* Phinney also bought herself tickets to Saint-Hilaire to join Babu and Lakpa at the festival, where she struck deals on their behalf with several gear companies, including Niviuk and Sup'Air, for additional photos and blogging content in exchange for some new paragliding gear. At the same time, David Arrufat attempted to negotiate potential sponsorship deals for Babu, often with the same companies Phinney had just talked to. Neither of them had much success, even though *Hanuman Airlines* won two awards at the festival: the Golden Icarus (the top film prize at Coupe Icare), as well as the People's Choice Award. Arrufat and Phinney did not leave on good terms, either.

After the Coupe Icare festival, Pevec sent *Hanuman Airlines* to America with Phinney so she could transfer the film over from the original PAL format, which he had made it in for the French festival, to high-definition NTSC, for submission to North American film festivals.† Phinney recut the film with the help of another American filmmaker friend and gave herself the title of executive producer in the credits. She then submitted it to the Banff Mountain Film Festival; it was eventually accepted into the Banff Mountain Film Festival World Tour.

Phinney claims that Pevec "gave" the film to her, and that she was told that Pevec, Davida, and Mukti "had no more time, and [that] none of them want to spend their own money on this."

Pevec says this isn't true. "I gave her all the source files, copied the whole project to a separate hard drive and shipped it off to her. So in that sense, yes, I did give it to her—but under the expectation that she was only going to export it onto full HD in a professional-quality

---

* The other publications that mentioned Babu and Lakpa's expedition did so on their websites and simply posted a selection of the four "free" photos Phinney had provided for them to use—a common practice in the magazine world, where editorial online budgets are close to zero.

† Although VHS video format is the same throughout the world, the electronic signal that is recorded on the cassette varies from country to country. NTSC is the standard used in North America and most of South America. PAL is the predominant standard used everywhere else, including Nepal.

studio, because we were in Nepal and didn't have that." Regardless, somewhere amidst the growing miscommunication, Phinney thought the film was now hers to start pitching to film festivals.

"I was told I stole the movie," Phinney says. "How can I steal something that was given to me?"

"I had this long, dreaded conversation with her over the phone, which I recorded for legal purposes," Pevec says. "Because she had threatened to sue me multiple times, and threatened to sue APPI. She took out a credit card in APPI's name, without permission. Using the APPI name to do shit with regards to the film. That was really early on too. It was one of those things, like, 'Whoa, whoa, wait. Who said you could do this?' She just took a lot of liberties like that. She acted like she was the lead on the project, but that clearly was not the case."

A long string of strongly worded e-mails was exchanged among Phinney, Pevec, Davida, and Mukti. Tensions rose. Babu and Lakpa distanced themselves from the situation as much as they could. They eventually asked Phinney not to return to Nepal and requested that she and David and Mukti stop selling *Hanuman Airlines* altogether. Everyone agreed. Pevec, meanwhile, continued to sell the film on his personal website and filled out a bulk order to *Cross Country* for 500 copies.*

It wasn't until November 11, 2011, that Babu and Lakpa were nominated for National Geographic's Adventurer of the Year Award. Phinney told them the news via Skype. They had no idea what she was talking about. They learned that they had actually won the award on February 10, 2012, during their interview at Sarangkot, still not really knowing what they had won. On February 28 *National Geographic* officially announced them as the people's choice for the award in a blog post on the website. The news was posted along with a series of ten photos and the edited two-and-a-half-minute video of the interview

---

* At the time of publication, *Hanuman Airlines* was still available for purchase on XCmag.com, as well as Pevec's personal website, Fauxreelfilms.com.

Alex Treadway had shot with them at Sarangkot eighteen days earlier. The post read:

> *With nearly 72,000 votes cast, we are thrilled to announce the 2012 People's Choice Adventurers of the Year: Nepalis Sano Babu Sunuwar and Lakpa Tsheri Sherpa. Their dream to complete the Ultimate Descent—climbing Mount Everest, paragliding down, then kayaking to the sea—truly embodies the spirit of adventure.*
>
> *Babu, 28, a kayaker and paraglider, and Lakpa, 39, a mountain guide, combined their skills to persevere in extreme conditions. Babu had never done a high-altitude mountaineering expedition like this before. Though he had three Everest summits to his name before the expedition, Lakpa didn't know how to swim, let alone kayak the Class V rapids they would encounter. Through teamwork and tenacity—and without the support of corporate sponsors or big budgets—they did something no one had ever done before.*

It was only after this announcement that the *Nepali Times* actually ran a short article about their trip—eight months after they had completed it. Babu and Lakpa, though, were still confused as to what, exactly, they had won. They still didn't have anything to show for what they had done besides a short, bad movie and a few even shorter magazine pieces with their names in them. And, in Lakpa's case, a large bill.

"To be honest, we are disappointed," Babu says. "We have this saying in my village: 'You can hunt all day for deer but only get a monkey. You don't even want to eat a monkey, but you must eat it, because you have worked so hard for it.' We have killed a monkey, I think."

The two friends went on to start their own paragliding company in Pokhara together later that same year. They called it Flying Himalayan Paragliding. It's doing well and making a small amount of money for them. Babu is in the process of teaching his wife, Susmita, and his brother, Krishna, how to fly. They each also had a new son in 2012.

Lakpa named his Sanga Dorjee Sherpa. Babu named his youngest Himalaya. Life goes on.

⸺ ⸻

Standing on a hillside on his family's farm in the Khumbu, Lakpa plants kiwi vines beneath the shadow of the mountains, waiting for the climbing season to start up again. The vines will grow on a wooden trellis he has constructed out of sticks, which he has dug into the ground along the length of a narrow terrace his ancestors carved out of the hillside long ago. The sky is cobalt blue and bright. The forest around him is dark and green, even in the sunlight. Below him, the valley seems to drop off into nothingness just past the edge of the kiwi terrace he's planting. The surrounding hills are steep, blocking his view of the icy ramparts of the higher Himalaya just to the north. He knows he will be walking slowly up them again soon. The climbing season on Everest isn't far away.

He plans on selling the fruit he is planting to tourists in Lukla, once it grows. He will call them "Sherpa Kiwis," he says, and will walk with the produce on his back a half hour into town each week to sell it.

"I am not special," he says later, reflecting on his and Babu's expedition, thinking of how a kiwi farmer who couldn't swim and a kayaker who couldn't climb somehow managed the impossible. How they flew off Everest and then paddled to the sea.

"I set a challenge for myself, and that's the important thing," Lakpa says, interpreting both the meaning and reasoning behind what he and Babu had done. "I don't want to tell my children what to do with their lives. I want to show them. I want to show them that whatever they want to do—they must do it."

ACKNOWLEDGMENTS

This book exists because of the amazing feats, generosity, insight, and patience of others—many others. First and foremost, I am indebted to both Lakpa Tsheri Sherpa and Sano Babu Sunuwar, who, after climbing Everest, flying off of it, and paddling to the ocean, somehow managed to not only survive, but sit cheerily through countless hours of tedious interviews with me. It is a feat beyond reckoning. Their kindness, patience, and bravery know no bounds.

Almost everyone included within the pages of this book went out of their way to assist in the making of it, particularly (in alphabetical order by first name) Alex Treadway, Balkrishna Basel (Baloo), Charley Gaillard, David Arrufat, Erik Boomer, Hamilton Pevec, Kelly and Nim Magar, Kili Sherpa, Kimberly Phinney, Krishna Sunuwar, Mahendra Thapa, Pete Astles, Phu Dorji Sherpa (Ang Bhai), Ryan Waters, Shri Hari Shresthra, Susmita Sunuwar, Wildes Antonioli (Mukti), and Yanjee Sherpa. This book would not have been possible without their assistance.

Many people not included within the text also played a vital role in my ability to report it, including (in alphabetical order by first name) Anup Gurung, David Michael Smith, Grayson Schaffer, Lalit Tamang, Mark Gunlogson, and Sagar Poudyal. Each provided valuable logistical support and sound practical advice that I would have been lost without. To Sagar Poudyal, in particular, I owe an extreme debt of gratitude for helping me arrange numerous key interviews in Nepal, oftentimes bringing me to them himself, with me sitting white-knuckled on the back of his motorcycle. No words would be on these pages without him.

This book wouldn't be what it is without the help of my fellow writers Eugene Buchanan, Joe Glickman, and Jon Turk, who all helped me in drafting the initial proposal. Similarly, I owe many thanks to

Falcon's former senior acquisitions editor John Burbidge, who initially accepted it and had enough faith in the story and myself to send me to Nepal to report it. Thanks are also owed to editor Katie Benoit and copyeditor Sarah Zink, who significantly polished the story and consistently provided sound practical advice through each stage of the drafting process. Additional thanks to Jeff Moag, editor at *Canoe & Kayak* magazine, for publishing the first article I wrote about Lakpa and Babu's expedition.

I, of course, was influenced greatly by the published work of others, namely (in alphabetical order by title) *Buried in the Sky: The Extraordinary Story of the Sherpa Climbers on K2's Deadliest Day,* by Peter Zuckerman and Amanda Padoan; *Dark Summit: The True Story of Everest's Most Controversial Season,* by Nick Heil; *Fallen Giants: A History of Himalayan Mountaineering from the Age of Empire to the Age of Extremes,* by Maurice Isserman and Stewart Weaver; *Ganga: A Journey Down the Ganges River,* by Julian Crandall Hollick; *Hell or High Water: Surviving Tibet's Tsangpo River,* by Peter Heller; *The Himalayan Database: The Expedition Archives of Elizabeth Hawley,* by Elizabeth Hawley; *Himalayan Whitewater,* by Peter Knowles and Darren Clarkson-King; *In Cold Blood,* by Truman Capote; *Into Thin Air,* by Jon Krakauer; *Life and Death on Mt. Everest: Sherpas and Himalayan Mountaineering,* by Sherry B. Ortner; *Nepal in Transition: From People's War to Fragile Peace,* by Sebastian von Einsiedel, David M. Malone, and Suman Pradhan; *The Snow Leopard,* by Peter Matthiessen; and *The State and Society in Nepal: Historical Foundations and Contemporary Trends,* by Prayag Raj Sharma.

During the drafting process I came to rely on the clear-sighted advice of several trusted readers: Dave Shively, managing editor at *Canoe & Kayak,* provided remarkably detailed line edits on each chapter draft; Kyle Dickman, a remarkably talented writer, read through each chapter and provided consistent direction; Brandon Keinath, a wizard by all standards, not only provided thoughtful line edits, but helped keep me in good humor—a great trick when writing your first book; Guenther Hobart looked very closely at every word, whether I wanted him to or not . . .

Heartfelt thanks are owed to my parents, Tom and Wendy, as well as my brother and sister-in-law, Ryan and Rachel, who have always stood by me and supported me in my own adventures.

Lastly, I'd like to thank the love of my life, Natasha, who has proved to be not only my harshest critic, but also my best editor, staunchest supporter, and greatest friend. This was all for you, you know.

INDEX